ISLAMIC
METALWORK

ISLAMIC METALWORK

Rachel Ward

Published for the Trustees of the British Museum by
British Museum Press

© 1993 The Trustees of the British Museum

Published by British Museum Press
A division of British Museum Publications Ltd
46 Bloomsbury Street
London WC1B 3QQ

British Library Cataloguing in Publication Data
A catalogue record for this book is available from the British Library

ISBN 0-7141-1458-8

Designed by Grahame Dudley Associates
Phototypeset in Sabon by Southern Positives and Negatives (SPAN),
Lingfield, Surrey

Printed in Italy by New Interlitho, SpA, Milan

FRONTISPIECE Brass bottle engraved with benedictory inscriptions and inlaid with silver (fig. 53). HT: 31.4 cm. Khurasan or the Punjab, c.1200.

FRONT COVER Detail of Venus in Taurus from the astrological cycle on the side of a sheet brass penbox (fig. 62), engraved and inlaid with silver and copper. Mosul, mid 13th century.

Contents

PREFACE

Islamic metalwork is spread across many countries and more than thirteen hundred years, and a book of this size cannot attempt to cover every aspect of such a rich and varied tradition. Rather than narrow the geographical area covered, I have chosen to concentrate on the early period, from the beginning of Islam in the seventh century to the end of the fifteenth century. This is not intended, however, as a value judgement, for there are magnificent examples of Islamic metalwork produced after 1500.

Most of the objects illustrated here are in the British Museum, which has one of the finest collections of medieval Islamic metalwork in the world. Much of the inlaid metalwork, including twenty-one objects from the collection of the Duc de Blacas (sold in Paris in 1866), was acquired between 1866 and 1896 under the direction of Sir Augustus Wollaston Franks (1826–97). He gave many objects himself and also encouraged a number of nineteenth-century collectors of Islamic metalwork, notably the antiquary John Henderson (d. 1878) and the architect and designer William Burges (d. 1881), to bequeath their collections to the British Museum. The collection has continued to grow during this century. Funds provided by Mr. P.T. Brooke Sewell (d. 1958), a merchant banker interested in oriental antiquities, have enabled many gaps to be filled, and much of the non-inlaid metalwork of the first centuries of Islam has been acquired through his generosity.

Inevitably gaps remain and a number of pivotal pieces, essential to a general introduction to the subject, are in other collections. Individuals and institutions who have kindly allowed me to illustrate objects in their collections are listed at the end of the book, but I would personally like to thank Kjeld von Folsach, Anatole Ivanov, Marlia Mango, Anthony North, Bernard O'Kane and

Yanni Petsopoulos for their help in obtaining photographs. I would also like to thank Edmund de Unger for making his collection available to me and the photographers and for his hospitality throughout our visit.

A book of this sort is founded on the work of others. Information and ideas have been drawn from a variety of sources and, in the case of translations of texts or poetry, often quoted verbatim. Some of the most important books and articles are listed as further reading on pages 124–5, but there are many other publications as well as unpublished lectures, personal communications and conversations which cannot be thus acknowledged. However, I am particularly indebted to James Allan, who first stimulated my interest in Islamic metalwork, and to Michael Rogers for years of constructive argument, and thank them both for reading and commenting on the typescript. I am also grateful to Susan La Niece and Paul Craddock of the British Museum Research Laboratory for much technical information and for their helpful comments on chapter 2, and to Jessica Rawson for her observations on the original outline of the book and for many thought-provoking discussions on metalwork generally.

The book itself owes its existence to a large number of long-suffering people. I would like to thank Peggy Ashenden, Yvonne Ashcroft, Renee Wyatt, Mary Bagulay, Lay Leng Goh, Carol White, Samantha Cooper, Claire Randell, Christine Wilson, Jane Newson, Christopher Kirby, Nathan Edwards, Elizabeth Adey, Jessica Harrison-Hall, Venetia Porter, Jane Portal, Carol Michaelson, Richard Blurton, Anne Farrer, Sheila Canby, Wladimir Zwalf, Robert Knox and Jessica Rawson, my colleagues in the Department of Oriental Antiquities, and Shelagh Vainker (ex-colleague), who have been tremendously helpful and supportive – processing photographic orders, ferrying objects, supplying Chinese and Indian analogics and providing innumerable other services. Other colleagues who have helped me with objects and advice include Christopher Entwistle, Jonathan Tubb and Donald Bailey. David Gowers and John Williams shot the marvellous new photographs which make even the most familiar objects appear fresh and exciting, Ann Searight created the evocative line drawings and map, Susanne Atkin compiled the index, and Grahame Dudley produced the beautiful design. Above all I am grateful to my editor, Nina Shandloff, who kept her promise and worked tirelessly to create a book from a typescript.

Finally, many thanks to Nick, Anna and Zöe Ward for their understanding and support throughout the writing of this book.

NOTE   *Transliteration has been simplified throughout.*

— 1 —

WHAT IS ISLAMIC METALWORK?

Islamic metalwork encompasses the metalwork of countries which have been temporarily or permanently under Islamic rule since AD 622, the first year of the Islamic era (see map on pages 122–3). There were distinctive metalworking traditions in the individual countries and towns within this vast area, but the Islamic religion influenced their development, giving them a common cultural identity which justifies their inclusion in a single volume. However, the term Islamic is used here in its widest sense, for this is not a book about the metalwork of a religion. Most of the objects to be discussed were intended for secular use, and no doubt some of the craftsmen, and indeed their patrons, were not Muslims.

The major categories of Islamic metalwork include vessels and utensils, jewellery, arms and armour, tools and scientific in-struments. All of these have separate traditions – different crafts-men and workshops, demands and techniques. This book deals only with the first of these categories: the functional and often luxurious vessels and utensils found in the Islamic household. These included lighting devices, such as lamps and lampstands, lanterns, candelabra and candlesticks; furniture such as large trays and tray stands which acted as mobile tables around the house; table and kitchen wares such as bowls, cups, dishes, jugs, ewers, cauldrons, saucepans, mortars and ladles; ewers and basins for ablutions; buckets for liquid soap, to be used in the bath; and

1 OPPOSITE Tray of sheet brass inlaid with silver and gold. The name and titles of the Mamluk sultan Shaʿban I (1345–6) are boldly inscribed around the tray and inside each medallion. Much of the inlay is now lost, but the design remains impressive. The radiating shafts of the letters resemble the rays of the sun, reminding visitors to the palace of the glory of the sultan. DIAM: 96 cm. Cairo or Damascus, 1345–6.

rosewater sprinklers and incense burners for perfuming the house or the person.

These essentially domestic objects have a particular standing within Islamic culture because of the absence of two categories of metalwork which, in other cultures, normally take precedence: figural sculpture and liturgical vessels. It is impossible to imagine a history of European metalwork, for example, without Donatello's David, images of the Crucifixion or chalices and patens, or a survey of Indian metalwork without figures of the Buddha or deities such as Shiva and Vishnu, bells, *lotas* and other ritual vessels.

Figural sculpture was condemned by Islam. It was too reminiscent of the icons of Christianity, Buddhism and other religions which Islam sought to replace. The Quran says: 'O believers, wine and arrow shuffling, idols and divining arrows are an abomination, some of Satan's work'. Religious authorities claimed that on the Day of Judgement painters and sculptors would be called to breathe life into their images, and would be eternally damned for usurping the creative function of God. Zoomorphic objects were produced 3 but their functional purpose, for example as furniture supports or containers, ensured that they were not worshipped as idols.

Liturgical vessels were not necessary to the Islamic religion. Metal objects were used in mosques, but only as items of furniture. They are usually indistinguishable from their secular counterparts, although some objects such as mosque lamps borrowed a sig- 2 nificance beyond their function from pre-Islamic cultures, and others, such as Quran holders, acquired one through association and continual use in a religious context.

Museum displays give the impression that Islamic metalwork consists almost entirely of highly decorated brass vessels, but this is a trick of survival. The literary sources frequently refer to gold and silver vessels, furniture and jewellery, and miniature paintings of 7, courtly scenes are full of such items. Islamic gold and silver objects have not survived in any quantity because the religion forbids the burial of goods with the dead. Above ground, precious metal was melted for profit at times of need, or reworked to more fashionable designs. Cultures famous for their goldsmiths' work invariably have an elaborate burial tradition: we would have little knowledge of pharaonic Egyptian goldsmiths' work, for instance, without the pyramids and other royal tombs.

Most surviving medieval Islamic gold and silver comes from hoards of treasure buried for safe-keeping by the owners, and for 16, some reason never collected. The necessarily random discovery of 38 such hoards gives only a patchy picture of precious metal in the medieval Islamic world. The richness of goldsmiths' work is best

2 Mosque lamp of pierced brass. The inscription around the rim, reading 'In the name of God', would have been thrown into silhouette by the light from inside. These lamps were hung in mosques and were visual reminders of a verse in the Quran: 'God is the light of the heavens and the earth; the likeness of His light is as a niche wherein is a lamp'. Similar lamps were used in Byzantium to mark holy places (see fig. 28). HT (without chain): 26 cm. Iran, 10th century.

conveyed by the treasury material preserved in the Topkapi Palace in Istanbul. It represents only a tiny fraction of the sultans' possessions when the Ottoman empire was at its height, yet it gives an overwhelming impression of the lavishness of court metalwork, with gold vessels worked into the most elaborate shapes and encrusted with emeralds, rubies, rock crystal and other precious materials in a display of extravagance that makes a twentieth-century visitor reel. The aesthetic represented by these objects was typical of the most lavish court goldsmiths' work throughout the Islamic period.

3 Incense burner in the form of a standing lion, cast brass pierced and inlaid with silver and copper. The head of the animal was removed to fill its body with hot coals and incense; the pierced walls enabled the scented smoke to escape. The owner's name, 'Ali ibn Muhammad al-Taji, is inscribed in kufic and inlaid with silver on the breast. The other inscriptions contain benedictions. HT: 45 cm. Khurasan, 11th century.

4 Bowl forged from high-tin bronze, with punched and engraved decoration. The colour and rarity of high-tin bronze made it a worthy alternative to gold and silver for those with strict religious beliefs or who were unable to afford precious metal. DIAM: 33.7 cm. Ghazni, 11th century.

5 Flask of sheet gold worked into elaborate repoussé palmette designs, set with a carved jade plaque and encrusted with emeralds and rubies. The flask contained drinking water for the sultan and was carried by an attendant behind him on ceremonial occasions. The unusual shape derives from leather flasks. HT: 28 cm. Istanbul, *c*.1560.

Our knowledge of simple utilitarian objects is also poor. There must have been an enormous amount of the undecorated, functional metalwork essential to domestic life, such as roughly constructed water carriers and cooking pots. Few of these have survived as they were melted for scrap when the receptacles were broken or discarded. Excavations of urban sites provide examples of this metal underclass, but many more excavations are needed before we can assess the range of this type of material.

Elaborately decorated base metal vessels often escaped the fate of metalwork either more or less precious. They were too fine to melt down for scrap and yet not fine enough to melt down for profit. Of course they were mended, adapted, amalgamated, the decoration added to, erased and often in the case of inlaid metalwork picked out, but they still survived and now form the bulk of existing Islamic metalwork.

Like many religions, Islam disapproved of the trappings of wealth. However, gold and silver have always been used in mosques and holy shrines and gifts were encouraged. Nasir-i Khusraw, writing in the middle of the eleventh century, describes the furniture and fittings in gold and silver which furnished the Kaaba in Mecca, the holiest site in the Islamic world, including silver-plated doors, door rings, six silver *mihrabs* with gilt and nielloed decoration, and silver mosque lamps. The donors of these riches were named on large silver plaques attached to the walls.

Condemnation was directed at the hoarding of precious metal for personal use. The Quran says:

Those who treasure up gold and silver, and do not expend them in the way of God – give them the good tidings of a painful chastisement, the day they shall be heated in the fire of Gehenna and therewith their foreheads and their sides and their backs shall be branded: 'This is the thing you have treasured up for yourselves; therefore taste you now what you were treasuring'.

The *Hadith* (collected traditions attributed to the Prophet Muhammad) are more explicit in their prohibition of gold and silver vessels. One claims: 'He who drinks from a silver vessel will have hellfire gurgling in his belly'. Another describes a Companion of the Prophet being offered water in a silver cup which he threw to the ground, saying: 'The Messenger of God has forbidden me to drink from a vessel made of gold or silver'.

Strict Muslims did shun vessels made of gold and silver. Al-Maʿarri, a tenth-century poet from Aleppo, is typical of these when he writes:

6 Inkwell of cast brass inlaid with silver and copper. Geometric designs and good wishes for an anonymous owner, written in different scripts, cover the exterior of the vessel. Scribes were often theologians, which may explain the lack of figural decoration on this object. The rings enabled the inkwell to be suspended from three cords when carried. HT: 9.8 cm. Khurasan, 12th century.

A clay jug for thy drink assign: thou'lt wish
Nor silver cup nor golden vessel there.

But these outbursts of disgust only emphasise the extent to which the religious ban was ignored by those with the wealth and inclination to use precious metalwork.

Inevitably there were moments of confrontation. The four-teenth-century traveller Ibn Battuta illustrates the pragmatic solution adopted on one occasion when he describes a banquet at the home of a Persian amir, at which food was served in gold and silver bowls, while glass vessels and wooden spoons were provided for the more scrupulous guests.

Against this sort of background, households could use base metal and other humble materials with honour, and perhaps even some sense of pious self-satisfaction. The eleventh-century scholar al-Biruni claimed that high-tin bronze, which can have the appearance of silver, was invented in the eighth century in response to the ban on gold and silver by the Umayyad caliph al-Hajjaj. This is not true, since high-tin bronzes are known from pre-Islamic times, but it does suggest that there was a market for metal alternatives to gold and silver. A similar desire to stay within Islamic law may lie behind the enthusiastic adoption of inlaid brass and, later, tinned or gilded copper. Religious authorities remained divided on the amount of gold and silver inlay permissible on an object, but inlaid brass was certainly considered more acceptable than solid gold or silver.

7 & 8 Double-page frontispiece from a copy of the *Khamsa* of Nizami, showing a banquet taking place in a garden by night. On the left-hand page servants prepare food for the waiting courtiers (on the right). A calf is slaughtered, bread kneaded and rolled, and cauldrons are heated over fires and their contents ladled into bowls piled ready for use. Opposite this scene of frenetic activity, the guests sit calmly listening to music, drinking wine from small cups and assuaging their hunger with fruit from a large bowl placed in front of them. Gold and silver vessels (the silver now tarnished and black) such as candlesticks, trays, bottles, cups and bowls are used alongside blue and white porcelain bottles and bowls.
19 × 12.5 cm. Herat, AH 898/AD 1493.

Figural decoration, like sculpture, was condemned by Islam for being too similar to the icons and idols of earlier religions. Although the Quran contains no specific statement on this subject, religious disapproval of figural decoration was established early in the Islamic period. Animals and human figures almost never appear in designs on furniture or other items used in mosques or shrines, and were also shunned by strictly orthodox Muslims. Although the quantity of surviving objects with extensive figural decoration demonstrates that the ban was widely ignored, it had a profound effect on all the arts, undermining the importance of figures in the decorative schema and discouraging realism. Conversely, it promoted the use of alternative designs such as arabesque scrolls, geometric motifs and inscriptions. Written Arabic, Allah's chosen method of communication through the Quran, became the Muslim equivalent of the figural cycles and icons which conveyed the message of Christianity and other religions. Calligraphy, the art of beautiful writing, was a highly honoured profession, and inscriptions were varied and ornate.

Although Islamic metalwork was made primarily for secular use, it was influenced by religious strictures in a number of ways, ranging from status and survival to the use of alternative materials and designs. This cultural background was common to the entire Islamic world; however, the creation of a distinct style was the accomplishment of the metalworkers, in conjunction with the patrons who commissioned or bought their works. The contributions of these two groups will therefore be examined next, followed by an historical survey of the metalwork of individual countries and areas.

9 OPPOSITE Box of cast brass engraved and inlaid with copper. Images of the planets and the zodiac have been adapted to exclude figures, presumably for religious reasons. Jupiter in Sagittarius, for example, normally an archer shooting at another figure, is reduced to a pair of hands cut off at the wrists. The bands of benedictory inscriptions demonstrate the variety of calligraphic styles used to decorate metalwork.
DIAM: 23.5 cm.
Khurasan, 12th century.

— 2 —

CRAFTSMEN, PATRONS, METALS AND TECHNIQUES

An understanding of the organisation of the metal industry and the metals, manufacturing and decorative techniques available to the craftsmen helps to explain why Islamic metalwork looks different from that of other cultures. Information is given both by medieval authorities and the objects themselves.

CRAFTSMEN

The complex iconographical cycle of the Vaso Vescovali or the poem extolling the virtues of the Tiflis ewer (see page 77) could only have been composed by literate and cultured craftsmen. Historians occasionally mention goldsmiths or coppersmiths who held minor government positions, traded as merchants or were members of the religious classes, and professional qualifications appended to signatures confirm that craftsmen could be well educated. However, details of the lives and careers of individual metalworkers are virtually unknown. They rarely signed their work, and even when they did there is little chance of finding them mentioned in historical texts or biographies – they were not sufficiently important.

Metalworking, like many medieval crafts, was a family business. Simone Sigoli, a fourteenth-century Italian pilgrim, attributed the skill of Damascus craftsmen to their family relationship:

The order they have among them is a beautiful and noble thing,

10 OPPOSITE The 'Vaso Vescovali', a lidded bowl of high-tin bronze decorated with complex astrological imagery and inlaid with silver. Twelve roundels around the bowl each contain the personification of a planet with the sign of the zodiac representing its day or night house. For example, the figure drawing water from a well is Saturn in his night house, Aquarius; the figure riding a ram is Mars in his night house, Aries. The lid bears images of the planets alone (see fig. 57). HT: 21.5 cm. Khurasan, c.1200.

for if the father is a goldsmith, the sons cannot ever have a trade other than this, and so they go from generation to generation so that of necessity they must be perfect masters of their arts.

Outsiders could also be taken into the business, usually as junior apprentices to learn the skills of the craft and to help with the more menial tasks. The signature on a candlestick reads: 'decorated by Muhammad ibn [son of] Fattuh of Mosul, the inlayer, apprentice of al-Shujaᶜ of Mosul', suggesting that the inlayer was trained by Shujaᶜ ibn Manᶜa of Mosul, the craftsman responsible for the Blacas ewer.

Within the industry, craftsmen had particular specialisations. The candlestick mentioned above was probably both designed and inlaid by Muhammad ibn Fattuh, but it was made by Ismaᶜil, who is also mentioned in the inscription. The Bobrinski bucket is also signed by both the maker, Muhammad ibn ᶜAbd al-Wahid, and the decorator, Masᶜud ibn Ahmad of Herat. Manufacturers and decorators might further specialise in a particular metal, technique or type of object, and sometimes their speciality forms part of their name, such as the coppersmith, the caster, the bucket maker, the engraver and so on.

Craftsmen could be workshop-based or itinerant. Most worked in urban centres where patronage was readily available. Whole streets or even entire quarters of cities were devoted to specific crafts and were filled with workshops, stores and shopfronts. The specialities of a town often became well known: the incense burners and mirrors of Hamadan, the drinking cups of Siirt, and the inlaid vessels of Herat, Mosul and Damascus are all mentioned by medieval writers.

For practical reasons, casting usually took place within a workshop. It involved unwieldy pieces of equipment including a furnace, bellows, moulds, a lathe to finish the object, large amounts of metal and fuel as well as a number of specialist craftsmen. However, some special commissions were undertaken by itinerant metalcasters. A huge object such as the water tank made for the shrine of Ahmad Yasavi at Yasi, north of Tashkent, would have been cast on site (as church bells were in Europe), as it would have been impossible to transport the finished vessel. The craftsman responsible for the casting was from a family of metalworkers in Tabriz, some three thousand kilometres to the west. Cauldrons and other large objects may also have been made by itinerant founders.

Goldsmiths and others working with precious metal, such as inlayers, could travel more easily. They worked with few tools, in small groups or alone, and the metal was generally supplied by the

11 Candlestick of sheet brass decorated with scenes of courtly life and inlaid with silver. The owner is anonymous but it is signed around the base of the neck by *al-hajj* (the pilgrim) Isma'il and Muhammad ibn Fattuh, who was trained as an inlayer in Mosul. HT: 34 cm. Mosul or Damascus, mid 13th century.

12 Large water tank of brass or bronze cast in sections: the seams of the joins remain visible. The tank was commissioned by Timur and made by the master 'Abd al-'Aziz, son of the master Sharaf al-Din of Tabriz, for the shrine of Ahmad Yasavi at Yasi in Transoxania in AH 801/AD 1399. HT: 158 cm, DIAM: 243 cm. Yasi, 1399.

13 Goldsmith's box of painted wood, containing a variety of steel balances, weights and tools decorated with simple gold overlay within special compartments of a removable tray. The three sets of balances come apart. The largest one has a tall shaft which screws into the wooden tray, thus forming a stand, and its two hemispherical pans are hung from purple silk and metal threads. The cylindrical weights for this balance are arranged according to size at the back of the tray, and each has a small knob for easy removal. Further smaller weights are stored beneath a hinged steel cover. Two smaller balances are contained within separate rectangular boxes with weights appropriate to their size. Other instruments contained within the box include a pair of scissors, an extendable rule, a file, a pen, a combination lock, several tweezers, a divider, a compass and measuring spoons. Various empty boxes, including the large rectangular one in the front left-hand corner, held materials or additional tools, and there is further storage space below the tray. The box is painted with scenes of Qajar princes out hunting and other courtly or historical scenes. L: 64 cm. Iran, 19th century.

patron. Indeed, because they were notorious for fraudulent practices such as debasing gold or silver with a cheaper metal or plating base metal objects and passing them off as gold or silver, craftsmen were often required to work in the house of the patron. He would supply the precious metal, in the form of coinage or damaged or outmoded vessels, and would have it weighed before and after manufacture, but it was still safer to keep a close eye on the process to ensure that none went astray. For example, the Mamluk historian Maqrizi relates that when Qadi ʿAla al-Din ibn Arab, the *muhtasib* or overseer of market practices of Cairo, was asked to arrange for some vessels to be inlaid with silver from coins supplied by his bride, he summoned the inlay specialists to his house to work on the project. As *muhtasib*, he would have been acutely aware of the possibility of fraud.

Itinerant craftsmen seeking patronage were one means by which metalworking styles and techniques spread across the Islamic world. Mosul metalworkers, for example, are known to have moved south to Egypt and Syria in the thirteenth century, attracted, no doubt, by the wealth of the Ayyubid and Mamluk courts. The craftsmen did not always travel voluntarily: Timur is said to have taken craftsmen of Damascus and other towns he had conquered back to his capital at Herat and the Ottoman payrolls are full of Persians, Bosnians, Hungarians and Egyptians brought back from successful campaigns. No doubt they were sometimes willing hostages – a conqueror can appear a more hopeful source of patronage than the defeated ruler of a war-ravaged country.

PATRONS

Islamic metalwork includes the grandest court regalia, made in metropolitan centres by royal commission, and the humblest kitchen utensil, made in a provincial workshop for sale at the local market. The varying tastes of its patrons are reflected in its material, form and decoration.

At the highest level, the influence of a patron might be considerable. As we have seen, he was often intimately involved with the production of a precious metalwork commission. Goldsmiths might work in his house or palace, and there were frequent checks on his market workshop to guard against fraudulent practices. This enabled him to give detailed instructions to the craftsman about the decoration. For instance, he could supply samples of his name and titles, poetic verses or other messages that he wanted engraved in fine calligraphy. He might specify the scenes he wanted depicted or show examples of fashionable imports from China or elsewhere which he wanted copied.

14 Candlestick (the neck and socket missing) of sheet brass inlaid with silver and gold. The bold inscriptions contain the name and titles of Sultan Muhammad ibn Qalaun (1293–4, 1299–1341). The Mamluk sultans commissioned large quantities of inlaid candlesticks and other objects for private and ceremonial use. HT: 21.1 cm. Damascus or Cairo, 1320–40.

When valuable objects were ordered from a workshop in another city, even another country, details could be sent with the order to ensure that the craftsman incorporated the patron's desires into the design. Historians record that a hundred brass candlesticks inscribed with the sultan's titles, as well as fifty of gold and fifty of silver, and a thousand wax candles, were amongst the items ordered from Damascus by Sultan Khalil for the circumcision ceremony of his brother Muhammad in Cairo in 1293. No doubt a sample of the sultan's name and titles, written out in the best calligraphy, would have been supplied with the order for the craftsmen to copy, and his representatives would have ensured that the order was carried out as requested. This close involvement of the patron meant that the tastes of the upper echelons of society were truly reflected.

Patrons did not always have such a direct influence, even on objects made with gold and silver, and were rarely involved with the production of base-metal vessels. The majority were intended for sale at market, locally or abroad; indeed, sometimes they were sold as containers of valuable material such as perfume or oil.

15 Bottle of cast brass. Small bottles with funnel-shaped necks such as this one probably contained valuable perfume or oil. A stopper in the top could have been held in place by material wrapped over the aperture and secured on the projections, and the solid cast shape would have been virtually indestructible in transit. The striking shape is reminiscent of modern glass perfume bottles; like them, the contents were more valuable than the container. HT: 16 cm. Khurasan, 10th–11th century.

16 Jug and bottles from the Harari hoard, a large hoard of silver vessels found in north Iran. Decorative techniques used include repoussé, engraving and niello inlay. Vessels in this hoard demonstrate a variety of styles and none bear owners' names. They were probably made in several workshops and may have been acquired in Khurasan by a merchant intending to sell them abroad. HT (max): 20 cm. Khurasan, 10th–11th century.

The specialities of certain towns attracted merchants who would retail them in other cities. The Harari hoard of silver, found together in a pot in north Iran, may well be merchandise collected from the metalworking centres of Khurasan. The hoard contains luxurious vessels: seven rosewater bottles, including two pairs; six incense burners; two caskets; three drinking vessels; one bowl, a spoon and a large number of horse trappings. The lack of owner's inscriptions, the number of vessels of the same type and the different styles of the group make it unlikely that all were intended for a single individual. They were probably being taken west by a merchant when he was forced to hide his wares – and obviously never reclaimed them.

The decoration on metal wares intended for sale at market generally reflected popular taste. Benedictory inscriptions wishing prosperity, happiness and success to an anonymous owner were common, as were astrological images and other designs which were suitable for any purchaser. However, there were moments when a certain group was identified as the main market force, and the form and decoration of the objects adapted to their taste; for example, the Mamluk metalworkers were particularly alert to the needs and demands of their European patrons as **17** relayed back to them by merchant intermediaries, and the shapes and decoration of their products indicate their ultimate destination.

17 Small candlestick of cast brass inlaid with silver and gold. The shape of the candlestick and its coat of arms (possibly of the Boldu family of Venice) indicate that it was made for export to Europe. HT: 12.4 cm. Damascus, *c.*1400.

METALS

Gold, silver, copper, iron, lead and tin had all been used by metalworkers of the Middle East since well before the Islamic period. Islamic metalworkers added just one new metal in the fifteenth century – zinc, previously used only in its non-metallic form alloyed with copper as brass. Most of these metals were mined in various areas of the Islamic world, the richest source being the eastern province of Khurasan. The main exception was tin, which was imported, presumably at considerable expense, from south-east Asia until about the fourteenth century, when it was imported in larger quantities from Europe.

Metals could be used alone but, with the exception of gold and silver, whose monetary value set them apart, they were usually combined to form alloys. The most common alloy was brass: copper with zinc. 'Pure' brass – copper which was high in zinc, with only traces of lead and tin – was used for objects made from sheet metal; the zinc made it both malleable and golden in colour. 'Leaded' brass – copper which was high in lead as well as in zinc – was used for cast objects. Lead was cheaper than copper and zinc and so helped keep down the cost of thick-walled castings, as well as facilitating the flow of metal and adding weight to the finished object. Useful sources of metal for these alloys were old or broken vessels and pre-Islamic statuary.

Brass was the favourite base metal for fine objects throughout the Islamic period, but it was susceptible to verdigris, an unattractive, foul-tasting and poisonous metal disease aggravated by liquid and acidic material. It was not, therefore, a suitable material for table wares or cooking vessels unless covered by a protective layer, such as a thin coating of tin.

Bronze – defined technically as copper plus tin with little or no zinc – is virtually unknown in the Islamic period, with the exception of some special products such as mirrors. The dark colour and patina of some leaded brasses has resulted in misleading descriptions of them as bronzes. It is impossible to detect the composition of metal accurately from a visual inspection, but scientific analysis has shown that the vast majority of such objects have the high zinc content characteristic of brass; they have therefore been described as brasses throughout this book unless there is scientific evidence that they are bronzes. However, particular areas specialised in making vessels from 'high-tin' bronze (copper alloyed with 20–30% tin), commonly known as 'bell-metal' in the West because of the clear ringing sound it makes when struck. High-tin bronze was more expensive than brass, both because the tin was imported and because it was a difficult and labour intensive metal to work. It

18 Mirrors of cast brass or bronze. The flat side was polished to give a reflective surface. Large numbers of circular mirrors with relief decoration in Chinese style were produced from the mid 11th century, perhaps because sand casting was introduced at that time from the east. DIAM: 11–11.5 cm. Iran, 11th–12th century.

was also esteemed for its peculiar properties: a silver appearance, the ringing sound it made when struck and its immunity against verdigris.

Iron and steel – the alloy of iron with a little carbon – were used for vessels as well as arms and armour, according to contemporary authors, but they are both particularly susceptible to corrosion and few examples have survived from the medieval period. Like high-tin bronze, steel was greatly valued by its patrons. The Mamluk historian Qalqashandi, when discussing the materials preferred by scribes for their penboxes, says 'Brass is the most used, steel less so on account of its rarity and costliness. It is the prerogative of the highest ranks of leadership, like the vizirate and similar ranks'.

MANUFACTURING TECHNIQUES

Manufacturing techniques can be divided into two fundamentally different processes: the molten metal can be cast to the desired form, or the solid metal can be worked to shape by a variety of processes such as hammering, forging or spinning.

Casting

Several methods of casting were known to Islamic craftsmen, and are mentioned by medieval authorities on metalworking practices. Open-face moulds provided a simple method of casting small items with one flat side, such as belt-fittings or pendants; the mould was sometimes engraved (in reverse) in stone for the sake of durability. Sand casting, a process in which the two sides of an object are impressed into sand within metal containers, which are then fastened together for the pour, provided a fast and efficient method of reproducing objects.

19 Detail of a brass lampstand, cast in sections and soldered together. The stamped and engraved designs decorated the original wax or pottery model and so were reproduced in the casting, thereby saving both time and labour. HT (whole): 75 cm. Afghanistan, 11th century.

Piece moulds were probably the most popular method of casting more complicated shapes during the Islamic period. In this technique, a model of the metal object is built up from wax or another material (around a core if it is intended to be hollow) and covered in clay to form a mould. The dry clay is cut into sections enabling it to be removed without being destroyed, and the modelling material is disposed of. The core, if there is one, is anchored to the exterior mould by metal rods called chaplets before the molten metal is poured into the cavity. Islamic metalworkers often simplified the process by casting a vessel in several sections and soldering them together, rather than designing a complicated piece mould capable of holding the whole object.

Cire perdue or the lost-wax casting technique, commonly used in the great bronze casting traditions of antiquity, was also known to Islamic metalworkers. The process is similar to that for piece moulds, but the mould is not in sections. The model is removed by melting the wax and pouring it out. The mould must be broken in order to remove the finished object and so cannot be reused. It is difficult to distinguish an object made by the lost-wax technique from one made in a piece mould, but the simple and repetitive forms of most Islamic metalwork suggest that piece moulds were normally used. The lost-wax technique would probably have resulted in greater variety and experimentation with shape.

The most curious feature of Islamic cast metalwork is that the technique is so little exploited. The main advantage of working with cast rather than sheet metal is that the thickness of the body can be varied to create interesting relief decoration, yet most vessels produced during the Islamic period have the smooth shapes characteristic of sheet metal. This phenomenon may be explained by the dominance of the gold and silver metalworking tradition. A patron thwarted in his desire for precious metal wares often wanted to imitate them as closely as possible in whatever material he could afford. For reasons of economy, gold and silver vessels were invariably hammered from sheet, and so a preference developed for

20 Ewer in the form of a cow suckling her calf with a lion crouching on her back, in cast brass engraved with figural scenes and inscriptions and inlaid with silver. This unique object, cast in one piece, must have been produced by the lost-wax technique, and the rather boastful inscription on the head and neck emphasises the importance of this achievement. It reads: 'This cow, calf and lion were all three cast simultaneously . . . on the order of Ruzba ibn Afridun ibn Burzin. Blessing to its owner Shah Burzin ibn Afridun ibn Burzin. Work of ʿAli ibn Muhammad ibn Abu al-Qasim the decorator in Muharram 603 [August 1206]'. HT: 35 cm. Iran, 1206.

the taut, flaring profiles typical of hammered metalwork. These shapes are reflected in many of the cast brasses. Indeed, these brass imitations are often our best source of information on the types and forms of precious metal objects which have not survived.

The most innovative cast brasses are those for which no gold or silver model existed. These include large objects, whose size made it impossible to use sheet metal and impractical to use cast gold or silver, or humble vessels such as cauldrons, mortars and bottles. For these the makers were free to exploit the sculptural possibilities of the casting technique.

Sheet metalworking

Simple objects can be constructed from sheet metal without additional work, apart from the soldering or rivetting of the joins. Basic utilitarian objects were often made in this way. Finer objects involved additional techniques such as hammering, spinning or turning.

Hammering was used to shape objects. They could be raised by hammering the metal sheet against an anvil, or sunk by hammering the sheet into a depression. Hammering was also used on objects made by another method such as spinning, in order to strengthen the rim or create a more elaborate shape. Hammered metal

21 ABOVE LEFT Vase for flowers, of cast brass with engraved decoration. The fluted body, narrow relief strip around the neck and wide flaring rim imitate sheet-metal vessels of gold or silver. HT: 20.3 cm. Khurasan, 10th–11th century.

22 ABOVE Jug of sheet brass. The golden colour of the brass, the faceted body and the intricate silver inlay create a luxurious effect comparable to that of its precious metal model. The animated inscription around the rim contains blessings for an unnamed owner. HT: 15.3 cm. Herat, c.1200.

33

23 Spun and hammered sheet-brass candlestick, decorated with blessings and animal friezes and inlaid with silver and a black material. The spinning technique would have reduced the manufacturing time for the base of this candlestick from over an hour to just a few minutes. The chuck could be reused to produce other bases of the same dimensions. HT: 29.8 cm. Mosul or Damascus, second half of the 13th century.

becomes increasingly brittle when worked and so needs to be annealed (heated) at regular intervals.

Spinning was chosen as a faster, more mechanical method of shaping an object, by pushing a disc of metal against a chuck rotating at great speed on a spinning lathe. The technique requires a considerable amount of force, and could not have been used before the invention of the cranked lathe. The first evidence of spinning can be seen in objects made at Mosul in the early thirteenth century, apparently the earliest use anywhere. The technique probably evolved to speed up the production of sheet-brass objects, but it is obviously only suited to regular concentric forms. Spinning is easily confused with turning, the finishing of an object on the lathe, which was a technique commonly used on both cast and sheet metalwork

23

from the Iron Age on. Both techniques leave a centring mark on the vessel, and this has often led to misinterpretation.

Forging, the alternative working and quenching of red-hot metal, was a method of manufacturing for high-tin bronze and iron. Both metals could be cast, and iron could also be worked cold, but high-tin bronze is brittle and susceptible to shattering if hammered when cold.

DECORATIVE TECHNIQUES

Much of the appeal of Islamic metalwork lies in its surface decoration. Even the most complex forms may be covered in minute decoration which challenges the three-dimensionality of the object. Traditional techniques were exploited to the full.

Designs were formed on the surface of the metal by repoussé, piercing, engraving and chasing. Repoussé – hammering the metal from inside the vessel against a firm but yielding material such as bitumen – created a relief design which could be extremely 52 elaborate (this technique was restricted to thinner sheet-metal objects). Piercing, the removal of metal to make holes in the object, made the piece visually and literally lighter, which could be an advantage for larger objects. Engraving, the removal of some metal from the surface with a sharp chisel, enabled the metalworker to create figural and other designs which could rival the pictorial arts in their complexity and detail. Chasing, the incising, punching or tracing of the surface without the removal of any metal, added 24 texture and detail to the decoration. This sort of surface decoration was sometimes mass-produced by applying these techniques to the 19 model of a cast object.

Colour was added to the metal surface by encrustation, overlay or inlay techniques. Encrustation, the setting of gems and other materials to form a relief effect on the surface of the object, was 5 employed primarily for the grandest court regalia. Overlay, the application of another material such as gold (gilding) or tin 83 (tinning) to the surface of the object, was often used in attempts to imitate gold and silver vessels.

Inlay, the laying of materials into the metal, was particularly popular in the Islamic period. Precious metals were often inlaid with niello (a hard, shiny black substance made from a mixture of metallic sulphides) to enhance their engraved designs. Base metals were inlaid with gold, silver and copper to add colour or black material such as bitumen to give contrast to their increasingly complex engraved designs.

The technique of inlay was skilled and time-consuming. For wire inlays, a series of tiny grooves were cut along the lines of the design,

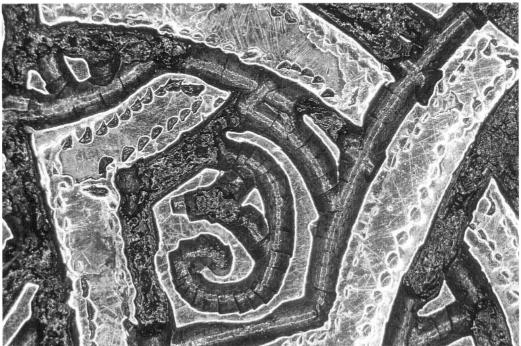

which had been lightly chased onto the object. The wire was then laid along the line of these grooves and hammered into the depressions. For sheet inlays, the edges of the area to be inlaid were undercut. The sheet was cut to shape and laid in place, and the lip of brass hammered down over it. The thin metal sheet was then usually chased with details of the design. The area around the inlaid design was often roughened and covered with a black material – bitumen, resin or even grime.

Islamic metalwork reflects the society which produced it. The lifestyles, preoccupations and aspirations of patrons are most ostentatiously expressed in the intrinsic value and function of their objects, and more subtle messages are communicated through the decoration. In many cultures painting, with its rich visual detail, is the best source for such information. Islamic painting, however, is virtually unknown before the thirteenth century and is generally restricted to manuscript illustration. Engraved metalwork, technically capable of almost as much detail as painting, was not tied to a narrative for its content, so the choice of decoration can be very revealing. Whether decorated with the astrological motifs of Ghurid Herat, the genre scenes of Zengid Mosul or the titular inscriptions of Mamluk Cairo, rediscovering the meanings these objects held for those who used them can greatly enrich our knowledge of the societies which inspired them.

24 OPPOSITE Detail of the 'Blacas ewer' (see fig. 59), with scenes from the life of the aristocracy of Mosul. On the left a lady admires herself in a mirror while her ugly maid stands ready with a casket of jewels. On the right a nobleman hunts deer using a cheetah trained to sit on the rump of his horse until prey is spotted. Mosul, 1232.

25 OPPOSITE BELOW Inlaid brass bowl viewed under high magnification. The silver wire has been hammered into parallel tracks of punched pits and the background gouged out to receive blackened pine resin. Damascus, 15th century.

— 3 —

CONTINUITY AND CHANGE

600–900

By AD 700, less than a century after the foundation of the Islamic era in 622, the Islamic empire stretched from the Bay of Biscay to the river Indus, and from the Aral Sea to the lower cataracts of the river Nile (see map on pages 122–3). It encompassed the whole Sasanian empire and much of Byzantium and was larger than the Roman empire had ever been. This vast area was ruled by the caliphs, the successors of Muhammad – first by the Orthodox caliphs (632–61), who ruled from Arabia, then by the Umayyad caliphs (661–750), who had their capital at Damascus in Syria, and then by the ʿAbbasid caliphs (750–1258), who moved the capital to Baghdad in Iraq.

The first decades of the new era saw little change in the cultural traditions of the countries comprising the Islamic empire. A network of Arab governors were made responsible for the newly conquered territories in an attempt to maintain central control and, more importantly, to organise the collection of revenue from outlying provinces, but the speed of expansion ensured that this essentially political network was thinly spread. Members of the old administrative hierarchies retained their positions and the bulk of the population remained non-Muslim.

If Islam made little immediate difference to local cultural traditions, it did have an effect on the distribution of wealth. Non-Muslims were subject to harsher taxation than Muslims and so

27 OPPOSITE Incense burner of cast brass with scenes from the life of Christ, including the Crucifixion, in high relief around the exterior. The censer was swung from chains during religious services (fig. 63 shows one in use). From the monastery of Mar Muza al-Habashi, between Damascus and Palmyra. HT: 6.5 cm. Syria, 6th century.

their power of patronage was reduced. Their Arab overlords, who dominated the main sources of revenue and valuable raw materials, were inevitably more important patrons. However, the Arabs enthusiastically adopted many of the varied artistic traditions which they found. Like modern ambassadors, Arab governors furnished their palaces in the style of the country to which they were posted – both to impress local dignitaries and for the pleasure of owning fine objects unavailable at home.

Many of the countries which made up the new Islamic empire had strong metalworking traditions, rooted in their own cultures and quite distinct from one another. The continuity of these diverse traditions during the early Islamic period makes it necessary to look at individual metalworking areas separately.

SYRIA

The countries of the eastern Mediterranean had been important suppliers of fine metalwork to the Roman and Byzantine empires. The church treasure of Kaper Karaon shows that there was an excellent silverworking tradition in Syria in the century preceding the Arab conquest. Such treasure was looted or demanded in tribute by the Arab conquerors. Caliph ʿUmar (634–44) is said to have given a silver Syrian censer with figural decoration to the mosque of Medina, according to the tenth-century author Ibn Rusta. This must have been similar to the brass censer from the monastery of Mar Muza al-Habashi, which was a popular Syrian type at this time. Apparently the Christian subject matter was not a problem until 783, when the governor of Medina had it destroyed. Unofficially, however, such objects continued to be used by Arabs, and several examples have Arabic inscriptions invoking the blessing of Allah in kufic script of the ninth or tenth century.

The vessel types seen in the Kaper Karaon hoard, with the obvious exception of the crosses, were all adapted to secular use and recur throughout the Islamic period, particularly in Syria and Egypt where the classical and Byzantine traditions were strongest. Many of the decorative techniques and motifs also recur. The most important of these was the inscription frieze, which was to play such an important part in the decoration of Islamic metalwork. Indeed, the simple style of much Islamic silver, with engraved and sometimes nielloed inscriptions, must come from Byzantine tradition as neither inscriptions nor the niello technique were popular in Sasanian Iran.

The Umayyad court, based at Damascus in Syria between 661 and 750, may well have used Christian liturgical vessels such as chalices and patens at secular functions and banquets, in order to

28 OPPOSITE The Hama treasure, a hoard of silver, probably from the Church of Kaper Karaon near Antioch. It includes most of the standard Byzantine liturgical objects: chalices, patens, ewers, wine strainers, fans, lamps, spoons and crosses. They are raised or cast and include repoussé, engraved and nielloed decoration. Seventeen of them bear inscriptions naming their donors. The treasure may have been hidden to avoid looting by Muslim invaders in the 640s. North Syria, 6th century.

reinforce their image as conquerors of Byzantium. However, as the Islamic empire was large and growing, an enormous amount of booty, tribute and gifts was flowing in from east and west. No doubt the Umayyad pantry and treasury would have shown the same eclectic and somewhat haphazard conjunction of styles and iconography as is visible in their architecture and its decoration.

EGYPT

Egypt was renowned for its metal foundries during the Roman and Byzantine periods. During the centuries preceding the Islamic conquest, the cast metalwork of Egypt was exported to North Africa and across the Mediterranean to Europe, even reaching England where a bronze cauldron formed part of the Sutton Hoo burial in the early seventh century. A variety of vessel types were produced, including lamps, lampstands, incense burners, strainers, ewers, bottles, ladles, bowls, boxes, buckets and cauldrons. The decoration is often restricted to the form of the vessel; for example, arcaded or ribbed bodies and ornamental handles are common.

Egyptian metalwork appears to have declined dramatically during the early Islamic period. Egypt was seen as a revenue provider for the caliphate; the population was heavily taxed and in no position to order fine metalwork. The Greek population left after the fall of Alexandria in 642, and Islamic-Byzantine enmity made trade across the Mediterranean difficult. Tin, an essential element in the bronze alloy, previously imported from Cornwall and other European sources, became scarce.

The material evidence suggests that the Egyptian metal industry suffered a blow from which it did not recover. Certain vessel types associated with Egypt disappear, and the quality of vessels with the same function is markedly lower. By the eighth century the governor of Egypt was reduced to melting statuary to solve a monetary crisis. Egypt had to wait for independence under the Tulunids (868–905) and especially the Fatimids (909–1171) before the economy recovered and metal production was revived, and it is not until the ninth century that Egyptian metalwork is found across the Mediterranean once again.

IRAN AND IRAQ

Silver vessels produced within the Sasanian empire are amongst the most magnificent examples of metalwork ever made. These imperial banqueting vessels consist of ewers, bottles, cups, bowls and dishes decorated with images of the king and Dionysiac scenes of feasting, dancers and serving girls. They are hammered from sheet and decorated in repoussé, sometimes with additional cast

29

elements crimped into place. Details were added by chasing or engraving but, unlike Byzantine metalwork, this was not the main method of decoration and inscriptions are extremely rare.

The striking imperial imagery of these vessels appealed to Muslim rulers who had none of their own and perceived themselves as inheritors of the Sasanian tradition. The ancient Persian tradition of the *bazm* or imperial banquet, with wine, singing, dancing and other entertainments, was continued during the Islamic period and many of the vessels pictured here would have played a part in that ritual.

ʿAbbasid poetry describes with admiration the Sasanian or Sasanian-style vessels which were in circulation amongst the elite. Abu Nuwas (762–815), the most famous poet of the ʿAbbasid period, writes:

Wine circulated among us in a gold cup, which a Persian endowed with various representations; on its bottom *Kisra* [Sasanian king] and on its sides wild animals ambushed by riders with bows; wine reached as far up as their buttoned collars, and water as far as their headgear.

He describes a serving girl pouring wine:

She marries wine with water in golden cups full of representations which neither speak nor hear; they are the images of the sons of Papak [i.e. Sasanian kings], with a ditch in front of them and when there is wine over them, they are like armies drowning in a whirlpool.

Abu al-ʿAbbas al-Nashi, a poet writing at the end of the ninth century, describes images of girls inside a cup:

They are so attractive that you are ready to take them for beauties bending in a coquettish manner, as though coming out of tents; and when the wine is mixed with water and divides itself into fold and pearls, it would seem that the beauties have put on gold as a robe and pearls form a necklace on their breasts.

Such serving girls, amply endowed and leaning forward in high relief, often adorn Sasanian metalwork; they would indeed have caused the wine and water mixture to form droplets on the repoussé surface of the cup.

The vessels described were not only Sasanian 'antiques' but also contemporary products in similar style which arrived at the court as

29 Sasanian dish, silver gilt with relief decoration of Dionysus (the god of wine) and attendants. Individual elements were made separately and crimped into place; the undercut metal can be seen where Dionysus' head has fallen out.
DIAM: 22.6 cm. Iran, 3rd century.

tribute, gifts or booty. Tabaristan, along the Caspian Sea, which had negotiated vassal status with the Arab invaders, attempted to maintain Sasanian traditions and continued to supply the ʿAbbasid caliphate with silver vessels in Sasanian style just as it had previously supplied the Umayyad court. The decoration is flatter and more linear, and the crowded compositions do not attain the simple hieratical effect of earlier images, but the subject matter and many of the details of costume and pose are comparable to Sasanian wares. 29

It would be wrong to give the impression that the ʿAbbasid court appreciated only the vessels of earlier cultures. By the ninth century

Islamic culture had established its own identity; Baghdad attracted poets, musicians and craftsmen from all over the empire and soon became the artistic focus of the Islamic world. According to medieval historians, the court ate from gold and silver vessels encrusted with gems, and curiosities such as the gold and silver tree with mechanical chirping birds perched in its branches, which decorated the Hall of the Tree at the wedding of Buran and the caliph al-Mamun in 825, were not uncommon. Whether these accounts are exaggerated or not, the luxury of ʿAbbasid Baghdad became legendary and set the standard for court regalia throughout the Islamic period.

30 Dish, silver gilt with relief decoration of a banquet in Sasanian style (see fig. 29). Vessels depicted include a shallow wine bowl, two wine jugs in a cooler, a cooking pot hung over a fire and a water bottle made from animal skin. DIAM: 19.7 cm. Tabaristan, 7th–8th century.

45

31 Bird-shaped ewer of cast brass engraved and inlaid with silver and copper. The handle is missing. A kufic inscription around the neck of the bird gives the name of the craftsman, Sulayman, and the date of manufacture, AH 180/ AD 796–7. HT: 38 cm. Iraq, 796–7.

32 The 'Basra ewer', a cast brass jug with engraved decoration. An inscription around the rim states that it was made by Abu (or Ibn) Yazid in Basra in the year AH 69/AD 689. Although some scholars believe the engraver omitted the century and that the date should read AH 169 or 269 (equivalent to AD 785 or 882), the ewer remains important evidence of a fine casting tradition in southern Iraq during the early Islamic period. Basra, AD 689, 785 or 882.

One surviving example of the idiosyncratic objects enjoyed at court is a magnificent large ewer in the form of a bird. The zoomorphic form and the naturalism of parts of its body such as the vicious-looking talons and beak indicate a debt to classical antiquity, but it is not a recognisable species and the surface decoration, much of it unrelated to the form of the bird, is already typical of Islamic metalwork, particularly the bold kufic inscription around its neck.

A jug which states in an inscription that it was made in Basra indicates that there was a local casting tradition of high quality in Iraq during the early Islamic period. However, Iraq was primarily a ceramic culture. ʿAbbasid potters had developed luxury pottery wares which rivalled porcelain in their colourful glazes and decoration. Local glass makers were famous, exporting their wares throughout the Islamic world and beyond. The quantity of surviving dishes, bowls and cups in pottery and glass indicate that these were used in preference to brass if the patron could not afford gold or silver, unless the object was too large for the potter to manufacture.

THE EASTERN PROVINCES

The eastern provinces of the Islamic empire had strong metalworking traditions founded on the plentiful local supply of metals, including gold and silver, especially in the region east of the Oxus river, known as Transoxania (Arabic: Mavera al-Nahr). Once under Islamic control, they provided the caliphal courts at Damascus and then Baghdad with much precious metalwork.

Some was booty taken when the Arabs first invaded in the mid seventh century. Historians list the huge amount of gold and silverwork that was looted, including Chinese engraved and gilded bowls of the Tang dynasty and large silver idols. The small bowl decorated with an image of Nana, a goddess fused from classical and Indian sources, is just one example of the sort of wares that the Arab conquerors would have found.

Arab governors, appointed by the caliph, commissioned more metalwork from local workshops. Al-Tabari mentions Nasr ibn Sayyar, the governor of Khurasan, ordering wine jugs of gold and silver to be made as part of a gift to the caliph al-Walid ibn Yazid in 742 (it did him little good with the caliph, however, as he was executed the following year). ʿAli ibn ʿIsa ibn Mahan, another governor of Khurasan, sent the caliph Harun al-Rashid one thousand Turkish slave girls, each carrying a gold or silver goblet. A floor painting of female musicians in Qasr al-Hayr al-Gharbi, one of the Umayyad desert palaces, depicts a tall ewer with ovoid

3.

34 OPPOSITE Two drinking bowls forged from high-tin bronze, one hemispherical, the other boat-shaped. They now have a lustrous dark patina, but originally they would have shone like the precious metal vessels whose shapes they copy. L: 23.5 cm; 15.2 cm. Khurasan, 7th–9th century.

33 Silver bowl with repoussé and engraved decoration. One of a group of similar bowls made in Khwarazm in the 7th century. The multi-armed goddess riding a lion is Nana, a popular local deity. An inscription around the exterior rim of the bowl includes the date (according to the Khwarazmian calendar) of 700, equivalent to AD 658. DIAM: 12.4 cm. Khwarazm, 658.

body and flat spout of a type known from Khurasan, which may be an example of these diplomatic gifts.

This area also produced fine cups, bowls and jugs from high-tin bronze. Al-Biruni, writing in the eleventh century, records Muhammad ibn Tahir, governor of Khurasan (862–72), drinking out of a high-tin bronze cup which may have been similar to one of the vessels in the British Museum. Our knowledge of other base metal products at this time is very poor, although the Soghdian casting tradition is likely to have continued. It is even possible that some objects currently attributed to the tenth and eleventh centuries are actually older.

After nearly three hundred years of Islamic rule, the metalworking traditions of the various countries which made up the Islamic empire still remained distinct. Indeed, for this early period the main problem is often to distinguish between the metalwork of the Islamic and pre-Islamic periods. However, the nucleus of a new 'Islamic' style appropriate to all media, developed in ʿAbbasid Iraq during the ninth century, gradually spread outwards from the centre of the caliphate and was imitated in distant corners of the empire. Its impact on metalwork becomes more apparent during the following centuries.

— 4 —

The New Style

900–1100

The 'Abbasid caliphate was beset by power struggles during
the ninth century, and by the end of the tenth century it was
little more than a puppet institution controlled by the
Buyids. As the caliphate became weaker, it proved impossible to
maintain central control of the entire empire from Baghdad and
several autonomous states were established. Baghdad was no
longer the hub of the Muslim world, and rival centres of patronage
were established at the courts of these independent states. The
problem of differentiating between objects of Islamic and pre-
Islamic date, seen in the last chapter, changes to one of distinguish-
ing between objects made in different areas of the Islamic world.

Despite the fragmentation of the empire, a number of trends first
seen in 'Abbasid Iraq can now be identified in metalwork from
across the Islamic world. The most obvious is the increasing use of
Arabic inscriptions in the decoration. Pious invocations and
sometimes the name and titles of the owner in fine kufic script are
seen on objects from the eastern and western ends of the empire.
Zoomorphic objects become less realistic and are covered in
engraved designs. The inscriptions and other decoration are
closely related to contemporary textiles, which may have been one
of the most important conduits for the communication of ideas
about design.

During this period brass appears to have been the medieval

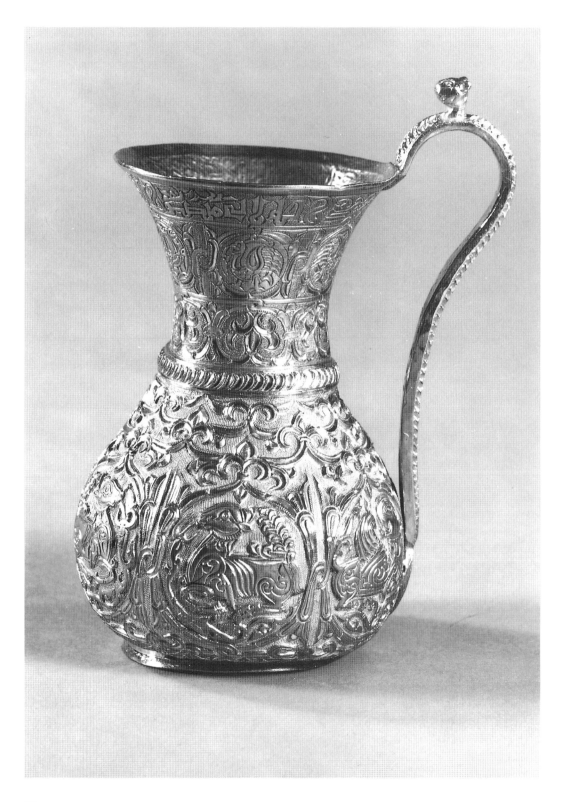

equivalent of a high-quality plastic – cheap, durable, strong, easy to mass-produce, but not fashionable. Gold and silver were relatively plentiful, but more important for base metalworkers, the Islamic potters and glassmakers had developed a range of products which provided serious competition to brass as alternatives to precious metalwork. Lustrewares, which successfully captured the metallic sheen of gold and silver, and white-bodied wares which emulated Chinese porcelain were extremely popular, as were the thin glass vessels which continued the skills of antiquity. Brass was limited to large objects such as ewers and lampstands which could not be made from the more fragile material, or functional objects for which the material was unimportant, or for which the additional weight and strength of the metal was an advantage.

This situation is repeated all over the Islamic world, wherever lustreware or other fine pottery was produced, and helps to explain why such a small number of prestigious brass wares have survived from this early period. The best brass wares were made in Khurasan, where a plentiful supply of metal and a strong metal-working tradition contrasted with a rather poor pottery industry; but even in Khurasan, really luxurious objects, such as candlesticks and rosewater sprinklers, were not made in base metal until inlaid brass became popular in the twelfth century.

IRAQ AND WEST IRAN

For most of the tenth and eleventh centuries Iraq and west Iran were ruled by the Buyids (932–1062), who entered Baghdad itself in 945, thereby gaining effective control of the caliphate. At its greatest extent their empire encompassed the whole of Iraq, and Iran as far north as Rayy and Hamadan and in the east to Kirman.

A gold jug or tankard commissioned by the Buyid ruler ʿIzz al-Dawla Bakhtiyar ibn Muʿizz al-Dawla (d.978) demonstrates the quality of metalwork at the Buyid court. The relief decoration and the animal images recall the finest Sasanian imperial metalwork. This was certainly intentional – the Buyids were conscious of their status as Persian kings, even claiming descendancy from the Sasanians themselves. However, the unnaturalistic treatment of the animal images and their subjugation to the overall design, in which the palmettes and inscription are given equal visual emphasis, represent a new aesthetic.

The shape of this jug, with its bulbous body, tall neck and everted rim, was popular for drinking vessels of all media through-out the Islamic world. It must have been one of a set of banqueting vessels used by ʿIzz al-Dawla Bakhtiyar. Part at least of such a set has survived in a silver hoard now in Tehran. Seven

35 Gold jug with repoussé and engraved decoration of birds and animals framed by scrolling palmettes on a ring-matted ground. The name and titles of the Buyid ruler ʿIzz al-Dawla Bakhtiyar ibn Muʿizz al-Dawla (967–78) are inscribed in kufic around the rim. HT: 13 cm. Baghdad, 967–78.

matching vessels inscribed with the name and titles of the amir Abu al-ʿAbbas Valkin ibn Harun, who has not been identified in the sources, give us an idea of the range of luxury tablewares used by a single individual in the later tenth century. The large salver would have been used to carry the smaller items, doubling as a table on a low stand or on the ground. The three bowls must have contained delicacies, as their sloping sides make them unsuitable drinking vessels; they would have fitted on the salver together and their inscriptions would have been easily visible at a low height. The two tankards, which have lost their handles, would have been filled with wine or water from the jug.

The austere decoration of these vessels, with their inscription friezes of titles and pious invocations on a ground of niello, relates the group to Byzantine silverwares, which had a long tradition of owners' inscriptions on precious objects. Indeed, the style of the calligraphy has been compared to stone inscriptions dated AD 984 and 1003 from north-west Iran, on the border of the Byzantine empire, and the amir and his silversmith may have been based in that area.

A gold bowl from a hoard found at Nihavand near Hamadan was owned by another military official. It was found with an assortment of silver gilt and nielloed horse trappings and weapon attachments, including a buckle bearing the name of the amir Abu Shujaʿ Injutakin. All of the objects in this hoard are small, light and easily transportable, well suited to a military man who travelled frequently. Verses around the exterior of the rim, ascribed to Ibn al-Tammar, a tenth-century poet from Wasit, indicate that the bowl was intended for wine:

Wine is a sun in a garment of red Chinese silk.
It flows; its source is the flask.
Drink, then, in the pleasance of time, since our day
Is a day of delight which has brought dew.

37 OPPOSITE Oil lamp for seven wicks, made of cast brass. A number of similar lamps have been excavated at Kish. The open dish shape and unusual handle relate them to stone lamps made in Iraq since the ʿAbbasid period. L: 27.8 cm. Iraq, 10th–11th century.

Our knowledge of Buyid base metalwork is very patchy, but a group of distinctive oil lamps provides important evidence for a continued tradition of fine cast brass vessels in Iraq. Mosque lamps with pierced decoration of inscriptions and geometric designs were also made within the Buyid empire and several fragmentary examples have been excavated at Rayy. However, this was a Byzantine type which was widespread by the Islamic period, occurring as far west as Tunisia. These must be copies of the silver and gold lamps, described by contemporary historians, that hung in important mosques and the holiest shrines. Nasir-i Khusraw

36 Drawing of a set of silver banqueting vessels, decorated with engraved and nielloed inscription friezes containing blessings and the name of the owner, Amir Abu al-'Abbas Valkin ibn Harun. Other vessels in the same hoard (not illustrated) do not bear his name but may have been used alongside this specially commissioned set. HT (tray): 37 cm. North-west Iran, c.1000.

38 Gold wine bowl from a hoard found at Nihavand in west Iran. A poem inscribed around the rim confirms that it was used for wine (see page 54). The engraved roundels and duck motif were probably inspired by contemporary textiles. DIAM: 7.6 cm. Iran, possibly Hamadan, 11th century.

describes a mosque in Jerusalem where 'they have hung many bronze and silver mosque lamps that burn every night'.

There is enough evidence to suggest a steady production of brass wares in Iraq and west Iran during the tenth and eleventh centuries. No doubt these were supplemented by locally made glass and pottery vessels, and by imports from the prolific metal workshops of Khurasan, as in the preceding centuries.

THE EASTERN PROVINCES

The eastern provinces of the Islamic empire gained effective independence from Baghdad in the ninth century. Local dynasties, notably the Samanids at Samarkand and Bukhara and the Ghaznavids at Ghazni, established courts which rivalled Baghdad as centres of culture and scholarship. Their access to the rich metal resources and strong metalworking traditions of this area ensured that some of the finest metalwork of the Islamic world was produced within their empires. The luxury of their courts is evoked by Gardizi, writing in the middle of the eleventh century, when he describes a party given by Mahmud, the Ghaznavid ruler:

It had been splendidly laid out, with extraordinary sweet-smelling flowers, delicious fruits, gems, a dinner service of gold and silver, crystal ware, mirrors, and other precious things.

Balkh was one of the most important silverworking centres at this time, located near the mountains of Panjhir (literally, five hills) which were mined extensively for silver. Indeed, Panjhir was sometimes described by medieval writers as Balkh's silver mountain. The silversmiths lived in a separate quarter of the city and had their own mosque. A flask made for a vizier in Balkh between 1030 and 1050 illustrates that one style produced there was quite plain, with simple engraved decoration. A number of other objects in similar style, preserved for the most part in the Hermitage Museum, can also be attributed to Balkh.

Ghazni was another important silverworking centre. According to Nasir-i Khusraw, it provided furnishings such as large silver door rings for the Kaaba in Mecca. The diversity of silverwork of this period suggests that there were a large number of centres. Just three examples from the Harari hoard of silver vessels found in northern Iran demonstrate the quality and variety of silverworking techniques and styles available at this time. The provenance and date of these vessels is difficult to ascertain – there may well be vessels of different dates and workshops in a hoard of this size (see page 28). However, the fact that a number of them can be related to later repoussé brass wares from Herat supports the tentative attribution of the vessels in this hoard to workshops in the eastern provinces operating in the tenth and eleventh centuries.

A large number of brass vessels are known from this area, probably because the metalworking tradition was so well established; however, the excavations at Nishapur, in eastern Iran, suggest that it was a relatively low-status material. Household objects found there include architectural and furniture fittings, kitchen wares, cosmetic utensils, lamps and ewers. The shaft from a lampstand, with fluted sides and pierced and engraved decoration, and a large cast ewer or jug are exceptional in quality of manufacture and decoration. Other metal objects are very simple and appear to have had a private or strictly domestic function. For example, the other seven ewers are simply constructed from sheet with only a little incised decoration around the neck. No brass tablewares were discovered – the only metal tablewares found at Nishapur were two lead bowls which must have been cheap (and poisonous) imitations of silver vessels. In contrast, the excavations have revealed large numbers of pottery bowls, dishes, jugs and other vessels. The residents of Nishapur obviously preferred to use the local pottery, with its monumental inscriptions or figural designs inspired by silverwares, if they could not afford a more luxurious material.

Brass vessels produced at this time are virtually all cast, but two

39 Silver flask with engraved decoration. The name of the vizier of Balkh, Shaikh al-ʿAmid Abu ʿAli Ahmad ibn Muhammad ibn Shazan, is engraved in kufic script around the body, punctuated by animals in roundels. A bolder kufic inscription on the shoulder contains anonymous blessings, which suggests that the vizier's name may have been added after purchase. HT: 25 cm. Balkh, 1030–50.

41 OPPOSITE (LEFT) Ewer of cast brass with extensive engraved decoration, one of the finest metal objects excavated at Nishapur. In form it derives from silver ewers made from sheet metal (see fig. 28 for a Byzantine example). Features such as the moulding at the neck, designed to strengthen the join of a sheet-metal ewer, are unnecessary in a cast vessel and the handle, which appears to have been applied, was actually cast with the body. HT: 33.5 cm. Nishapur, 11th century.

42 OPPOSITE (RIGHT) Bucket of cast brass with engraved decoration of racing animals and benedictory inscriptions on a ring-matted ground. The style of this bucket is similar to the Nishapur ewer (see fig. 41), and objects like these would have been used together for ablutions. Their size and function made pottery an unsuitable alternative, but wealthier households probably owned silver or even gold versions of these vessels. HT: 15 cm. Khurasan, 11th century.

40 Pottery bowl painted in slip under a clear glaze. The straight flaring sides and the dark calligraphy on a white ground imitate silver wares with nielloed decoration. DIAM: 34.6 cm. Nishapur, 11th century.

different approaches to form are evident. The first exploits the advantages of the casting technique with strong, sculptural, sometimes geometric forms, generally without additional surface decoration. This type includes a variety of vessels simply decorated with almond-shaped bosses. Small pear-shaped bottles are particularly common, but other bottles, incense burners and mortars also occur. The bosses added weight and strength to the fabric of the vessel.

The second imitates the hammered sheet-metal shapes of gold and silver vessels, and relies on surface effects rather than volume for visual impact. Indeed, these more pretentious vessels were probably highly decorated in an attempt to disguise their humble medium. Dimples and ribs punctuate the smooth surface of the vessels and provide a framework for the decoration of medallions and friezes containing foliate or knot motifs and inscriptions. Broader friezes were introduced in the eleventh century, often featuring animal processions and inscriptions in a variety of styles. These engraved brass wares were ultimately to inspire the use of inlay.

Objects with openwork decoration, generally in the form of linked palmettes or strapwork, form a subdivision of this group. The piercing technique was best suited to thin-walled sheet-metal objects, and so these pierced brasses may also reflect precious metal wares which have not survived. The style of kufic script on many of these pieces dates to the tenth century, although the style continued into the eleventh. Vessel types include vases on domed bases, lobed cups, ewers, lampstands and incense burners. Many of them are in the shape of animals, or have animal finials, legs or spouts.

Finally, a large group of vessels continues the established high-tin bronze-working tradition of the eastern Islamic lands. Al-Biruni, who was probably writing in Ghazni, the Ghaznavid capital, in the middle of the eleventh century, lists some of the objects made from high-tin bronze in his day as drinking vessels, water jugs, bowls and washing basins. The brittleness of the metal encouraged the use of domed punches to create patterns of indentations, but many of these esteemed vessels also bear finely engraved inscriptions and even figural designs.

EGYPT, SYRIA, NORTH AFRICA AND SPAIN

The Fatimids (909–1171) were the most important force in the western Islamic lands during this period. They first gained power in North Africa, but in 969 they conquered Egypt and established their capital in Cairo. From there they extended east into Syria and the Hijaz, although Egypt remained their base.

43 Bottles of cast brass decorated with almond-shaped bosses. These small bottles are the same shape as those used for bath oil by the Romans and probably had the same function. The bosses would have provided a good grip during an inevitably slippery operation.
HT: 12–13 cm. Afghanistan, 10th–11th centuries.

44 BELOW Brazier of cast brass with openwork decoration and lion-headed feet.
W: 12.5 cm. Khurasan, 10th–11th century.

Independence helped Egypt to regain some of its former glory. Trade with India and Europe and access to the gold mines of Africa brought enormous wealth, and the luxury of the Fatimid court in Cairo was famous. When the treasury was plundered in the mid eleventh century observers were amazed by the quantity of gold and silver furniture and vessels, many encrusted with precious stones. Amongst them were six thousand gilded silver perfume bottles, a large gold tree and a selection of toys. Nasir-i Khusraw, who visited the state apartments in the palace in 1046, describes the huge gold throne used by the caliph, which took up nearly a whole room and was as tall as it was wide. Three sides were of gold, decorated with hunting scenes – perhaps similar to the lively scenes depicted on Fatimid lustre pottery – and beautiful inscriptions. He also describes a gigantic silver chandelier commissioned by the sultan, which was so large that the doorway of the mosque had to be demolished to get it inside. Unfortunately, little Fatimid court art has survived. The treasury was burnt in 1062, then sacked by the Ayyubids when they conquered Egypt and ousted the Fatimids in 1169. Small items of jewellery are all that remain to illustrate the quality of Fatimid goldsmiths' work.

The Fatimids inherited the casting tradition of the eastern Mediterranean and many of the brass vessels produced during the Fatimid period continue pre-Islamic forms. This continuity can

45 Oil lamps of cast brass or bronze. The larger Coptic lamp has an ornamental handle and a hole in the base for a pricket lampstand. The later Fatimid lamp is smaller, thinner-walled and much simpler in design, although the figure of a naked man above the spout must be a throwback to the elaborate lamps of late antiquity. It has no hole for a pricket in its base and must have been put on a lampstand fitted with a flat tray (see fig. 46). HT: 20 cm; 5.3 cm. Egypt, 6th and 8th–10th century.

46 Brass lampstand, cast in sections. The striking star shape of the tray is repeated in the rim of the stand. HT: 58 cm. Egypt, 10th–11th century.

make it difficult to distinguish those vessels produced during the Islamic period from earlier examples of the type, particularly when they have no additional decoration. Two objects illustrated here have only recently come to light in various departments of the British Museum, and it is likely that in time the numbers of known Fatimid metal vessels will be further swollen by other currently unidentified objects lurking in museum basements.

However, the overwhelming impression from surviving vessels of the Fatimid period is that the metal-casting industry had declined during the first centuries of Islamic rule. Although the situation improved under the Fatimids, the brass industry faced intense competition from luxury wares such as gold, silver and rock crystal and, more directly, from the cheaper alternatives to those wares: fine pottery and glass.

The situation is well illustrated by a single type of vessel – the oil lamp. During the fifth and sixth centuries a large number of extraordinarily elaborate oil lamps were made in Egypt. These had a hole in the base for mounting on a special pricket lampstand. By the Fatimid period very few brass lamps were being made, and they were usually small insignificant objects. However, the number of pottery lamps had increased, and the spikes on the pricket lampstands had been replaced by flat trays to allow the pottery lamps (which could not be mounted on a pricket) to sit flat instead.

Surviving brass wares consist of simple functional objects and include very few bowls or other tablewares. This is in stark contrast to the large quantity of lustre pottery bowls and dishes decorated with lively figural scenes or inscriptions. The best brass objects are those which could not be made in pottery – lampstands, incense burners, large ewers, buckets, and furniture, including a splendid series of zoomorphic supports and fountain heads. These are often left plain, as they had been during the pre-Islamic period, but the most pretentious examples are engraved with fine kufic inscriptions, small birds and animals, vine scrolls or geometric designs.

Egypt was the most important power in the western Islamic world, and therefore probably produced the best metalwork and other crafts during this period. However, there were rival centres of patronage in the other Muslim countries around the Mediterranean basin. The Umayyads of Cordoba and their successors in southern Spain were enthusiastic patrons of the luxury arts. Gold, silver and brass vessels have survived in church treasuries in Spain along with ivories, textiles and other fine objects. Surviving brass objects from North Africa suggest that there were local casting traditions in several areas even after the Fatimids moved to Cairo.

Trade and cultural links existed between the different countries

47 Jug of cast brass, with a distinctive angular handle featuring a rectangular openwork section. This jug was obtained from a Coptic monastery in Egypt, but similar examples have been found in Sicily, Lebanon, Mallorca and Spain. HT: 16.5 cm. Possibly Egypt, 9th–11th century.

around the periphery of the Mediterranean, just as in late antiquity, and this often makes it difficult to assign a specific provenance to an object. Vessels of the same form have been found in Egypt, North Africa and Spain. They could either have been made in one centre and exported or in several centres with close ties to the others. It seems wiser to think in terms of a Mediterranean culture until the differences between the metalworking traditions of these countries have become clearer.

No object illustrates this situation better than the griffin of Pisa. The exceptional quality and unusual nature of this object should help in determining its provenance, but over the last twenty years it has been variously attributed to Iran, Sicily, North Africa, Egypt and Spain, and there is still no general agreement amongst scholars.

This monumental beast would have been a worthy ornament to

48 Ewer and bucket of cast brass. The ewer is undecorated but the bucket is engraved with a fine kufic benedictory inscription and an arabesque scroll. Vessels such as these were used together for ablutions. Their shapes can be paralleled in pre-Islamic Egypt in both silver and bronze. HT (bucket): 12.5 cm; (ewer): 28.5 cm. Egypt, 10th–11th century.

65

49 Silver casket with repoussé, gilt and nielloed decoration, made for Hisham II just before his accession in 976 and signed under the clasp by Badr and Tarif. The shape copies the finely carved ivory caskets popular at the Umayyad court in Spain and even their precious metal mounts are imitated, although these are actually hammered from the same sheet of silver as the casket itself. L: 38.5 cm. Cordoba, 976.

any palace. It must have supported a large and heavy object, possibly a fountain or candelabra, and there is space in the decoration of its rump to allow such an object to rest there. It stands more than a hundred centimetres high and was cast in one piece, the wings and tail (now missing) attached by rivets. The finely sculpted details of the head and body could only have been achieved by skilful casting, indicating a well-established tradition wherever it was made. The decoration of the griffin indicates the pre-eminent position of textiles at court. Its body is covered by the engraved equivalent of a silk saddlecloth, with roundels which in the original would have contained small animals, and a border of monumental kufic script containing benedictions to its owner. The true ability of the metalworkers can be seen in this animal, which is neither an imitation of a sheet-gold or silver object nor a simple functional vessel. No doubt the workshop which produced the griffin made others like it, and only by chance did this one survive atop a cathedral in Pisa.

50 The griffin of Pisa: a large griffin cast in four pieces, the wings and tail (missing) attached by rivets, and engraved with blessings in kufic and other designs. The griffin spent over four centuries atop the cathedral in Pisa. Suggestions for its place of manufacture have included Iran, Sicily, North Africa, Egypt and Spain, and its provenance remains controversial. HT: 107 cm. Egypt or Spain (?), 11th century.

51 Drawing of three polycandela from a large cache of light fittings discarded in a storeroom of the Great Mosque at Qayrawan, which included a mosque lamp in the name of the Zirid ruler al-Muʿizz (1015–61) signed by Muhammad b. ʿAli al-Qaysi al-Saffar (the brass worker). They would have been fitted with tubular glass oil lamps and hung from the ceiling of the mosque. DIAM: 30–34.5 cm. Qayrawan, Tunisia, 9th–11th century.

Despite the fragmentation of the empire, the Islamic religion and culture continued to be a unifying force during this period. A new style, established across the Islamic world, incorporated shapes and motifs, even iconography, from disparate earlier cultures, but it was now identifiably 'Islamic', and similar shapes of vessel and styles of decoration can be seen in objects from countries as far apart as Spain and Afghanistan.

— 5 —

THE GLITTERING
SURFACE

1100–1300

This was a very exciting period for all media, as craftsmen experimented with new techniques and designs in an attempt to fulfil the desire for surface ornamentation which had been growing during the first centuries of Islamic rule. The most important development in metalwork was the fashion for the inlay technique, which began in the eastern provinces during the twelfth century and soon spread west across the Islamic world. Inlay transformed brass vessels into luxury wares which could compete with gold and silver for the patronage of the wealthy. A wide range of decorative motifs evolved, so that the entire surface glittered with silver and copper designs. The sumptuous effect of these vessels invited comparison with contemporary gold and silver wares, and the similarity was made more striking by the use of sheet brass and repoussé ornament to expand the range and subtlety of shapes to be decorated.

Inlaid brass dominates our view of Islamic metalwork during these and the succeeding two centuries. It is therefore even more important to remember the quantity of other metalwork produced, which has not survived so well: gold and silver, whose position at the head of the metal hierarchy remained unassailable because of their monetary value, and non-inlaid base metals, which often imitated the shapes and decoration of the richer metal wares for less wealthy patrons.

52 OPPOSITE Detail of a sheet brass ewer inlaid with silver and copper (see fig. 56). The repoussé and inlaid decoration transform a base metal object into a glittering luxury vessel. The parakeets show particular skill and must have been worked from inside the ewer using a snarling iron. The inlaid decoration features medallions containing images of the planets, each with the sign of the zodiac representing its day or night house. Visible here are the moon in Cancer (the crab) and Mercury in Gemini (the twins). The human-headed inscription contains blessings. Herat, 1180–1200.

THE EASTERN PROVINCES

For much of the twelfth century the eastern provinces were a battleground for the Seljuks, Ghaznavids, Ghurids and other minor dynasties. Despite the political instability of the region, however, a large quantity of very fine metalwork was produced, culminating in the sheet-brass vessels inlaid with silver and copper that are amongst the most splendid examples of Islamic metalwork to have survived. These were made between about 1170 and 1220, particularly in Herat, one of the most important cities of the Ghurid empire.

The Ghurids (1148–1215) were chieftains from the mountainous district of Ghur, between Herat and Ghazni. They ousted the Ghaznavids from Ghazni in 1151, forcing them to retreat to Lahore. They made serious inroads into Seljuk territory in Khurasan and into Ghaznavid and Rajput territories in India before they were finally conquered by the Khwarazm-Shahs in 1215, just before the Mongol invasions which decimated the area for years. Ironically, the metalwork produced under Ghurid rule is often described as 'Seljuk', although the Seljuks were their political rivals.

The role of the Ghurid court in the development of inlaid brass is unclear. The names of Ghurid rulers and courtiers do not appear on the objects. On the contrary, most are inscribed with generalised blessings to unidentified owners, and those few with names include two which mention merchants from west Iran. This confirms a 54 claim made by Zakariyya al-Qazvini, the thirteenth-century cosmographer, that Herat was the centre of the inlaid brass industry and that inlaid brass was exported from there, and suggests that much of this fine metalwork was made for the export market rather than for local consumption.

External factors such as a shortage of silver, which forced both craftsmen and patrons to seek alternative materials, and an increasingly bourgeois customer base, which increased demand for pretentious but cheaper vessels, have been suggested as the impetus behind the fashion for inlaid brass. These may well have played a part, but inlay was also a natural development for Islamic metalworkers. The engraved decoration of brass vessels had become increasingly complicated, and by the twelfth century the 41 intricate designs covering the surface of these objects could be difficult to read. The use of inlaid metals of other colours helped to 54 clarify the designs.

Metal inlay was not new to the Middle East; it had been used by Sasanian and Roman metalworkers and continued to be employed sporadically during the Islamic period. However, increased contact between Khurasan and northern India must have heightened

53 OPPOSITE Bottle of cast brass with goat-shaped handles, engraved with blessings in different scripts and inlaid with silver. The flask was acquired in the Punjab and may have been made in the Indian provinces of the Ghurid empire, as the form is unparalleled in Islamic metalwork and the squared foot relates to later Indian vessels. HT: 31.4 cm. Khurasan or the Punjab, c.1200.

54 OPPOSITE The 'Bobrinski bucket', cast brass inlaid with silver and copper. An important inscription on the rim reads: 'Ordered by ʿAbd al-Rahman ibn ʿAbdallah al-Rashidi, made by Muhammad ibn ʿAbd al-Wahid, worked by *hajib* Masʿud ibn Ahmad the decorator of Herat, for its owner the brilliant *khwaja* Rukn al-Din, pride of the merchants, the most trustworthy of the faithful, grace of the pilgrimage and the two shrines, Rashid al-Din ʿAzizi ibn Abu al-Husain al-Zanjani, may his glory last'. The handle is dated Muharram 559 [December 1163]. The other inscriptions are blessings for an anonymous owner, suggesting that these vessels were designed for the market place, with any special inscriptions being added to the rim or the handle after purchase. The friezes of figural decoration include groups of musicians, revellers, huntsmen and an early depiction of two people playing backgammon. The visual clarity of these detailed scenes was achieved by the skilful use of three different-coloured metals in the design – brass, copper and silver. HT: 18.5 cm. Herat, December 1163.

awareness of the technique. Copper and silver inlays were used in Kashmir and north-east India in the eleventh and twelfth centuries to emphasise various features of idols, such as the eyes or the 'sacred thread' (symbolising the spiritual birth of the high-caste Hindu). Booty brought back from Ghaznavid and Ghurid sorties into India would have introduced Islamic metalworkers to this work, and Indian craftsmen may even have been employed in local workshops.

The development of the inlay technique can be traced throughout the twelfth century. Earlier examples use copper wire to frame the engraved decoration or to highlight important elements of the decoration such as inscriptions. The wire was inlaid into deep recesses and has survived well, although it does acquire a dark patina which can make it difficult to distinguish from the brass ground. Silver was being used alongside copper by the middle of the twelfth century, and by 1163, the date of the Bobrinski bucket, inlays appear throughout the decoration to produce a rich polychromatic surface.

By the last quarter of the twelfth century silver had virtually replaced copper in the decoration of the finest pieces, and a slightly different technique had evolved in order to lessen the cost of the precious metal. For linear inlays, wire was laid over a parallel series of small pits and hammered down until part of the wire was held firmly. For spatial inlays, metal sheet was laid over an area of which only the edges had been pared back, and these were then hammered down to hold it in place. Neither the wire nor the sheet inlays were deeply recessed, so much less silver was needed. The disadvantage of this more economical technique was that the inlay was considerably less secure, easily picked out or even falling out at a later date, leaving the parallel tracks or pared ground of the brass as the only evidence that the object was originally inlaid.

The development of the inlay technique revolutionised the status of brass vessels. The use of silver and gold inlays increased the intrinsic value of the object, and the wasting of the precious metals, which were not easily retrievable, gave it additional appeal for those inclined to conspicuous consumption. Inlaid brass became immensely fashionable, outstripping pottery and rivalling silver and gold as material patronised by sultans and the wealthy.

A range of prestigious objects, such as candlesticks and rose-water sprinklers, were made in brass for the first time and more time was spent on the manufacture of the vessel itself. The craftsmen turned to sheet metal in order to imitate more closely the finest gold and silver wares. The silver-workers themselves, who were skilled in the creation of complex sheet-metal shapes, may

55

55 Dish of sheet brass inlaid with silver. The dish was probably hammered into a mould to form the faceted shape. An example of this type of dish in silver in the Hermitage Museum emphasises the similarity between the manufacturing techniques of sheet brass and precious metal vessels at this time. L: 29 cm. Herat, c.1200.

have been responsible for the first examples. Of course, there had been earlier imitations of sheet-metal vessels in cast brass, but although these could emulate the shape, they could never attain the lightness and surface tension of a hammered object. Indeed, the greater strength of the brass material enabled metalworkers to elaborate on the silver prototypes, and the best repoussé ornament can be very fine. The ewer in the British Museum is a variation on the form of a silver ewer in the Hermitage Museum, which appears quite plain in comparison.

The novelty and value of inlaid brass vessels is conveyed by an exultant inlayer who inscribed another high-spouted ewer in the Tiflis Museum, dated 1181–2:

My beautiful ewer, pleasant and elegant,
In the world of today who can find the like?
Everyone who sees it says 'It is very beautiful'.
No-one has found its twin because there are no others like it.
Glance at the ewer, a spirit comes to life out of it,
And this is living water that flows from it.
Each stream which flows from it into the hand
Gives each hour new pleasure.
Glance at the ewer which everyone praises;
It is worthy to be of service to such an honoured person as you.
Everyone seeing how moisture flows from it
Is able to say nothing which is not appropriate to it.
This ewer is for water and they make it in Herat.
In what other century can they make the like of it?
Seven heavenly bodies, however proud they may be,
Are protection for the one who works so.
Let kindness come down on the one who makes such a ewer,
Who wastes gold and silver and so decorates it.
Let happiness come to him if he gives the ewer to a friend.
Let trouble come if he surrenders it to an enemy.

The poem suggests that the iconography of these vessels was deeply symbolic. The poet Nizami compared the source of life, concealed in the shadows of the land of darkness, to the source of the sun. How otherwise, he argued, would it be possible to drink of its waters, for it is the rays of the sun that make it drinkable? To a contemporary viewer, this ewer would have symbolised the source of life from which water flows and therefore also the source of the sun – the latter indicated by the fluted body and radial inscription around its neck (representing its rays) and the circling planets around its body. In this context, the depictions of real and imaginary animals, birds and fishes on the ewer represent the material and spiritual world. The benedictory inscriptions further increased the protective potency of the object.

The claim that Herat was the centre of the inlaid metal industry is borne out both by inscriptions on two of the finest objects, the Bobrinski bucket and the Tiflis ewer, and by the number of craftsmen whose names indicate that they lived or were trained in Herat. However, the cities of Merv, Nishapur and Tus also feature in metalworkers' names, so there may well have been other inlay centres within both the Ghurid empire and the empires of their rivals. A group of high-tin bronze bowls are decorated in rather different style to objects associated with Herat, and these may represent one alternative centre producing fine inlaid vessels.

56 RIGHT High-spouted
water ewer of sheet
brass with elaborate
repoussé decoration
and inlaid with silver
(see detail, fig. 52).
The benedictory
inscriptions and complex
astrological iconography,
such as the combined
images of the planets
and zodiac, were potent
talismanic symbols for
the owner and maker,
as is made clear by the
poem on the similar
Tiflis ewer (see page 77).
HT: 40 cm. Herat,
1180–1200.

57 Lid of the 'Vaso Vescovali' (see fig. 10), high-tin bronze inlaid with silver. The eight roundels contain personifications of the planets carrying emblems of their magical influences. These multi-armed figures must derive from Indian tradition, as does the addition of an eighth figure, the dragon Jawzahr, which represents the lunar eclipse. Khurasan, *c*.1200.

The inlay workshops flourished until the 1220s when Chingiz Khan and his Mongol army invaded Khurasan. Whole cities were razed to the ground and their entire populations slaughtered. Not surprisingly, the production of fine metalwork in this area seems to have ceased. However, the inlay technique travelled west with metal exports and also, probably, with craftsmen fleeing before the Mongols, and during the thirteenth century a number of inlay centres sprang up in Syria, western Iran, the Jazira, Anatolia and Egypt.

59 OPPOSITE The 'Blacas ewer', made of sheet brass (the spout and the foot are missing) hammered to form a faceted body, engraved and inlaid with silver and copper (see details, figs. 24 and 60). This magnificent ewer was decorated in the workshop of Shuja^c b. Man^ca in Mosul, which must have been one of the best in the city. Craftsmen trained by him and other Mosul masters ensured that the distinctive local style of inlay, with its genre scenes in friezes and medallions on geometric grounds, had a lasting influence in Mosul and elsewhere (see fig. 11).
HT: 30.4 cm.
Mosul, April 1232.

58 BELOW Box of sheet brass inlaid with silver. The inscription around the lid contains the name and titles of Badr al-Din Lulu, ruler of Mosul. The geometric ground is typical of Mosul work and may have been inspired by the Chinese silks which were traded in the city. HT: 10.2 cm. Mosul, 1210–59.

IRAQ

The dissemination point in the western Islamic world for the new inlay technique was Mosul, a prosperous city on the banks of the Tigris in north Iraq which had strong trading links with the east. A long period of control by Badr al-Din Lulu (1210–59), first as vizier of the last Zengids and then as an independent ruler, brought stability to the city, and the arts flourished. Badr al-Din Lulu himself actively supported the inlaid metalwork industry in his capital, and five vessels bearing his name and titles survive.

The most important example of Mosul metalwork is the Blacas ewer. An inscription around its neck reads: 'Decorated by Shuja^c ibn Man^ca of Mosul in the month of Rajab [April] in the year AH 649/AD 1232 in Mosul'. Despite the fame of Mosul's inlay work, this is the only object which states unequivocally that it was made there, and with the five objects (two trays, a candlestick, a basin and a box) made for Badr al-Din Lulu and a bowl made for one of his courtiers, it forms the core group of identifiable Mosul metalwork.

The inlay technique raised the value and status of Mosul brasswares just as in Khurasan. Luxury objects such as candlesticks were made in base metal for the first time, and many of these probably reflect local precious metal prototypes that have not survived. The craftsmen worked predominantly with sheet brass – the domed incense burners represent the only major group of cast brass vessels. Indeed, Mosul metalworkers seem to have been the inventors of the spinning technique (see page 34), which enabled them to respond much faster to the huge demand for inlaid brass vessels. Fine hammered pieces, with fluted bodies and other repoussé work, continued to be made, but the spinning technique encouraged the creation of smooth-walled circular shapes suitable for production on the lathe.

Although Mosul metalworkers borrowed the inlay technique from the east, most of the vessel forms and decorative motifs were drawn from a local repertoire. A comparison between the Blacas ewer and the ewer made in Herat less than fifty years earlier reveals the individual character of Mosul metalwork. Both vessels are hammered from sheet brass and inlaid with silver and copper, but there the similarity ends. The shape of the Blacas ewer, with its pear-shaped body, tall neck and long spout (now missing), continues a local tradition known from the Byzantine period (see fig. 28 for a spoutless version of the shape) which is quite different from the high-spouted type made in Herat.

The decoration is extremely varied, with a wider range than Khurasanian metalwork. Astrological, hunting, enthronement, battle, court and even genre scenes are all represented. Scenes of

60 Detail from the 'Blacas ewer' (see fig. 59). The left medallion depicts Bahram Gur out hunting with Azada, his favourite musician, in a scene from the *Shahnama*. To impress her, he tickled the ear of a deer with an arrow and as it scratched the itch he pierced foot and ear with a single arrow. On the right is a wealthy lady in a camel-litter. Contemporaries complained of jams caused by litters in the narrow streets of Mosul and of the noise of their tinkling ornaments. Mosul, 1232.

everyday life, such as the lady and her attendant riding on the back of a camel led by another servant, are characteristic of Mosul metalwork. Similar scenes were popular in contemporary book painting and there may have been a connection between the inlay workshops and book illustrators, but ultimately both were indebted to the genre tradition of late antiquity, which had resurfaced occasionally during the Islamic period – on Fatimid lustre pottery, for example.

Some of the decoration of the Blacas ewer was based on eastern models. One medallion has a depiction of Bahram Gur out hunting with his favourite Azada, in a story from Firdawsi's Persian epic the *Shahnama* or *Book of Kings*. This scene is unknown on earlier western objects, but does appear amongst the frieze of hunters around the base of the Vaso Vescovali. The animated inscription around the body also probably comes from Khurasan, where inscriptions inhabited by figures and animals were extremely popular. However, the effect of the decoration, with its clear divisions into roundels and friezes on a ground of simple geometric ornament, contrasts with the organic distribution of the decorative elements on the Herat ewer.

61 Incense burners of cast brass inlaid with silver (see detail, fig. 63). A verse on one reads: 'Within me is the fire of Hell but without floats the perfume of Paradise'. HT: 19–21 cm. Mosul and Syria, 13th–early 14th century.

62 BELOW Brass penbox with astrological decoration (see front cover) inlaid with silver and copper, and with an inscription from the Quran: 'I desire only to set things right so far as I am able. My succour is only with God; in Him I have put my trust'. L: 36.8 cm. Mosul, 13th century.

Mosul inlay work was renowned. Its products were exported for sale and as gifts to princes and other foreigners, according to contemporaries such as the geographer Ibn Saʿid, writing in the middle of the thirteenth century. This confirms that brass vessels had finally achieved sufficient status to compete with gold and silver for the most important and discerning patrons. Demand for inlaid brass attracted Mosul metalworkers to set up workshops abroad, and the technique and Mosul style of decoration soon spread to Syria, Egypt, west Iran and Anatolia, where many thirteenth- and fourteenth-century inlayers styled themselves 'al-Mawsili' (from Mosul) in their signatures.

In 1244 Badr al-Din Lulu submitted to Mongol suzerainty, and thus Mosul avoided the Mongol sacking suffered by so many other cities. His son was not so wise, however, and the city was plundered in 1261–2. The diaspora of Mosul metalworkers may have accelerated with the arrival of the Mongols in 1244; some were probably taken to their capital at Tabriz. It is unlikely that the industry survived the plundering of 1261, and objects signed by Mosul craftsmen or decorated in the Mosul style are usually attributed to other centres after that date.

SYRIA

A number of metalworkers had already left to seek the patronage of the Ayyubid sultans (1169–1250, Damascus until 1260) and their courts before the Mongols sacked Mosul in 1261. The Ayyubid sultan Salah al-Din (Saladin), who conquered the Fatimids in 1169, divided his empire between members of his family, and so separate Ayyubid dynasties ruled in Egypt, Damascus, Aleppo, the Jazira and the Yemen.

63 Detail of an incense burner (see fig. 61) showing a Christian ecclesiastical figure swinging a censer. Syria, late 13th century.

More than fifteen surviving objects bear the name and titles of an Ayyubid sultan. Some may have been exported from Mosul, but others must have been produced within the Ayyubid empire itself. The first object we can be sure was made in Damascus is a cast brass incense burner in the Aron collection. An inscription on the hinge states that it was made by Muhammad ibn Khutlukh of Mosul in Damascus. It is undated but must have been made during the second quarter of the thirteenth century, as a geomantic instrument in the British Museum by the same craftsman is dated AH 639/AD 1241–2. These two examples suggest that there was a casting workshop in Damascus that was capable of unusual and complex work.

The first sheet brass object to state that it was made in Damascus is a ewer in the Louvre dated AH 657/AD 1258, which was made by Husain ibn Muhammad of Mosul for the Ayyubid sultan Salah al-

Din Yusuf, who ruled from Damascus. The shape of its faceted body is similar to the Blacas ewer, so clearly vessel forms as well as the inlay technique and decorative style were carried south by the migrating Mosul craftsmen.

A group of metalwork decorated with Christian figures and events belongs to this period. Some of these may have been commissioned by Christians, but surprisingly, the iconography does not exclude the possibility of a Muslim patron – a basin and a tray made for Sultan Najm al-Din Ayyub, who ruled Diyarbakir (1232–9), Damascus (1239, 1245–9) and Egypt (1240–9), are decorated with Christian scenes. It has been suggested that these vessels symbolised Muslim superiority over the Christians, an understandable preoccupation during the period of the Crusades.

64 Basin of hammered brass inlaid with silver made for Sultan Najm al-Din Ayyub (1232–49). The sultan's titles, on both the interior and the exterior, suggest that the basin was made after he received the caliphal investiture in 1247. In addition to conventional sporting and battle scenes, arabesque ornament and inscription friezes, there are five scenes taken from the life of Christ: the Annunciation, the Adoration, the raising of Lazarus (seen here in the upper medallion), the entry into Jerusalem and the Last Supper. HT: 23.3 cm. Damascus, 1247–9.

WEST IRAN

Metalwork made in west Iran during the twelfth century is largely unidentified. Khurasanian metalwork was certainly imported – objects such as the Bobrinski bucket, made for a merchant from Zanjan, and a number of vessels in local museums testify to that. It is possible that objects currently attributed to Khurasan will prove to have been made in west Iran under strong eastern influence. The situation becomes a little clearer in the thirteenth century, but our knowledge is limited to a small number of objects, some of the highest quality, which defy attempts to define a chronology.

Given this situation, the inscribed silver bowl in the Keir collection is of paramount importance, as it can be dated and located with some precision. The inscription around the rim bears the name and titles of Badr al-Din Qarakuz (d.1219), whose career in western Iran included the governorship of Hamadan in 1194 and other high offices. The quality of the bowl strongly suggests that it was part of an established precious metalworking tradition in this area, of which the gold bowl from Nihavand may be an earlier example. The goldsmiths' market in Hamadan was well known during Hamid Allah Mustawfi Qazvini's lifetime, only a century later, and the bowl may have been commissioned there.

65 Silver-gilt bowl with repoussé gadrooned sides and engraved decoration made for Badr al-Din Qarakuz, named in the inscription around the rim. The decoration also features medallions of harpies and arabesques on a ring-matted ground. In shape the bowl is related to a type of footed bowl with domed cover known from Byzantine silverwork of the 12th century. DIAM: 20.7 cm. West Iran, possibly Hamadan, 1200–19.

Iran probably provided a home and work to some of the craftsmen fleeing Mosul after the Mongols conquered the city in 1261. Indeed, it is more than likely that craftsmen were taken, voluntarily or not, to work at the Il-Khanid courts. A hoard of inlaid brass vessels found at Baznegerd near Hamadan, including two signed by ʿAli ibn Hamud of Mosul (one dated 1274), is important evidence that the Mosul style penetrated Iran. A number of objects with elements of Mosul style which have often been attributed to Syria do not fit happily with metalwork known to

66 Brass tray inlaid with silver and gold which may have been made by Mosul craftsmen taken to the Il-Khanid court at Tabriz. DIAM: 46.3 cm. West Iran (?), late 13th century.

66

87

67 Caskets of cast brass inlaid with silver. The caskets illustrate the strong influence of the Mosul school, with friezes and roundels displayed against a geometric ground. The inscriptions are either ornamental or contain anonymous blessings. HT: *c*.13–14 cm. South or west Iran, 13th and early 14th century.

have been made within the Ayyubid empire, and they should probably be reattributed to Il-Khanid Iran. Several of them feature compositions and motifs which were to be developed further by Persian metalworkers in the fourteenth century.

Another style current in west Iran during the second half of the thirteenth century is represented by the small penbox dated 1281, one of the finest examples of the inlay technique from any period. It appears more strongly indebted to Khurasanian metalwork, with its fine linear style on a plain ground and its preoccupation with astrological motifs, than to Mosul metalwork which is usually bolder and more clearly defined. It may represent the continuation of an earlier style in west Iran, inspired by imports and craftsmen from Khurasan. An important feature of this penbox is that the copper inlay has been replaced by gold. This was to become increasingly common towards the end of the thirteenth century, although the main inlay material remained silver.

67

69,

71

68 Candlestick of cast brass engraved with courtly figures on each of its facets and inlaid with silver. A phoenix and running gazelles depicted in small panels on the neck mark the beginning of Chinese influence, brought by the Mongols when they invaded Iran from the east. HT: 23.7 cm. West Iran, late 13th century.

69 ABOVE Penbox of cast brass inlaid with silver and gold, signed under the clasp by Mahmud ibn Sunqur and dated AH 680/AD 1281. Fine interlace with animal-headed terminals covers the box, interrupted by medallions and roundels containing astrological figures, dancers, musicians and vegetal and geometric ornament. There are no inscriptions apart from the craftsman's signature, which is hidden when the clasp is closed. The seven planetary figures are depicted inside the lid (from left): the moon, Mercury, Venus, the sun, Mars, Jupiter and Saturn. The interior of the box has openwork decoration of musicians and animal interlace lined with coloured leather. The hinges and clasp are also in openwork. L: 19.7 cm. West Iran, 1281.

70 OPPOSITE (ABOVE) Detail of the top of the penbox by Mahmud ibn Sunqur (fig. 69). The exterior of the lid bears roundels in three groups of four containing symbols of the planets and the zodiac. Clockwise from the top of the central roundel are Mercury in Virgo (a double personification of the planet holding ears of corn), the sun in Leo (a sun rising behind the back of a lion), Mars in Scorpio (a warrior holding two scorpions by their tails) and Venus in Libra (a harp-playing lady seated beneath a set of scales).

71 OPPOSITE (BELOW) Base of the penbox by Mahmud ibn Sunqur (fig. 69). The extraordinary quality and lavishness of this penbox is proven by the beautiful decoration on its base, which would not normally have been seen. Two pairs of horsemen are shown jousting and hunting between three large roundels filled with intricate geometric designs. A frieze of swooping birds frames the decoration.

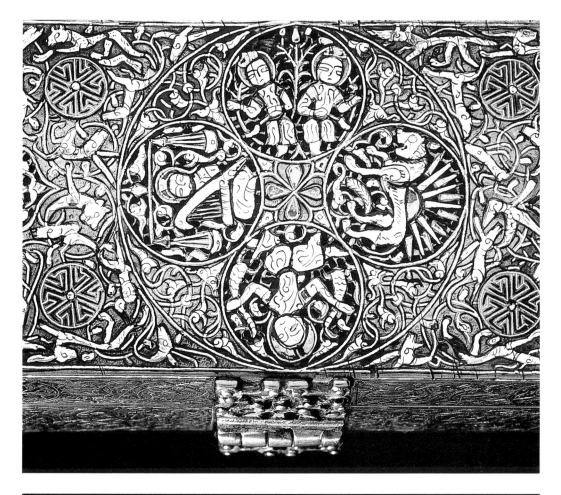

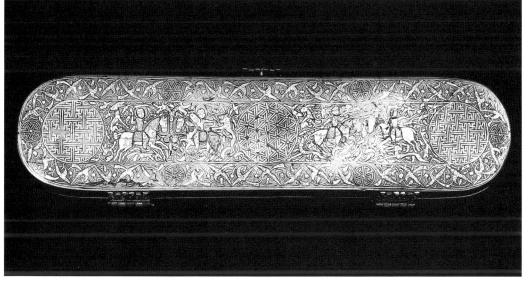

ANATOLIA

Another style which has been attributed to north Iraq and west Iran is now usually attributed to Konya in Anatolia. The majority of the objects in this group are cast brass candlesticks with distinctive concave bodies and sockets. The remarkable consistency in their shape contrasts with the tremendous variety of their iconography. The candlesticks illustrated here include one covered with small rosettes on a ground of knotted interlace, another with images of the planets and a third with large roundels of horsemen and friezes of courtly activities. Others in the group borrow images from Western iconography such as St George and the dragon or the seasons and labours of the months. This diversity of pictorial sources and apparent lack of concern about mixing styles is typical of the art and architecture of Anatolia under the rule of the Seljuks of Rum. The inlaid decoration of the earliest pieces is comparable to Mosul metalwork and may have been the work of migrant craftsmen from that city, but the type continued into the fourteenth century, when influence from Il-Khanid Iran is apparent in the chinoiserie style of decoration and more sophisticated figural compositions.

72 Candlesticks of cast brass engraved and inlaid with silver, demonstrating the variety of designs used to decorate them. HT: 20–2 cm. Konya, 13th–14th century.

The inlay technique spread rapidly across the Islamic world, adopted enthusiastically by craftsmen and patrons alike. Inlaid brass was not only an acceptable alternative for many who were loath, for religious or financial reasons, to use gold and silver vessels; its decorative qualities also made it fashionable with patrons willing and able to afford precious metal. Inlay enhanced the many figural designs, geometric and floral motifs and ornamental inscriptions which were popular on engraved metalwares, and encouraged even more complex and intricate designs. At this stage owners' names were rarely included in the decoration, which reproduced traditional themes and popular motifs. These pieces appear to have been made for a general (albeit wealthy) market rather than specific individuals or groups. However, the vessels made for the Ayyubid sultans indicate the direction in which inlaid brass was to go, with increasing influence being exerted on its style and decoration by powerful patrons.

— 6 —

POETRY AND PROPAGANDA

1300–1500

The fashion for inlaid brass, introduced during the previous two centuries, peaked during this period. Having become established as a serious alternative to gold and silver, it was now exploited by wealthy, sophisticated and powerful patrons. The Mamluk pieces, in particular, are dominated by inscriptions which trumpet the social position of their owner so loudly that the vessels seem intended more as vehicles of propaganda than for pleasure and appreciation. This sort of personal aggrandisement was appreciated in Iran also, but generally the Persian examples are more lyrical, with verses of poetry in place of titular inscriptions, and other decoration strongly influenced by manuscript illustration and Chinese imports. Both these styles reflect court taste, which was an increasingly important influence on inlaid metalwork at this time.

The situation changed during the fifteenth century as the price of gold and silver escalated and local patrons were unwilling to 'waste' the precious metal as inlays, which were difficult to retrieve. Inlaid brass became rarer and more sparing in the use of gold and silver, and metalworkers turned increasingly to the European market.

The decline of the inlay technique coincided with an increase in imported tin. Tinned copper alloy vessels became popular, the overlay of tin being applied to their interior and exterior surfaces. This technique effectively replaced inlaid brass as a cheaper metal

73 OPPOSITE Cup of high-tin bronze inlaid with silver and gold. The poetic inscription around the rim relates to the function of the cup as a drinking vessel (see page 100) and the decoration includes figures drinking and feasting. HT: 12.7 cm. Iran, 14th century.

74 Lantern of brass with intricate pierced decoration of arabesques and repetitive benedictory inscriptions. It is very similar to the pierced elements on North African bell-lamps, such as those still hanging in the Qarawiyyin Mosque in Fez. The layout and detail of the pierced decoration is also comparable to stucco work in buildings in Morocco and Spain. HT: 29 cm. Morocco or Spain, 14th century.

alternative to gold and silver, and it had a dramatic effect on the development of later base metalwork.

Spain and North Africa remained outside the mainstream of Islamic metalwork during this period. The inlay technique was not widely practised in the western part of the Islamic world, although the emphasis there on inscriptions and arabesque designs suggests 7. that they kept abreast of stylistic developments.

IRAN AND AFGHANISTAN

Ghazan, the Il-Khanid (Mongol) ruler of Iran, converted to Islam in 1295 and instigated a series of reforms to repair the damage caused by seventy years of Mongol mismanagement. His court at Tabriz became an enlightened centre of scholarship and culture, benefiting particularly from the interchange of ideas with China which was also under Mongol rule at this time.

Trade with China brought paintings, drawings, lacquerwares, textiles, porcelains, silverwork and even craftsmen to Iran, and their impact is clearly visible in the metalwork of the period. Chinese bronzes, however, were heavy cast objects with functions specific to their own society, and they were not generally exported. Persian craftsmen continued to use traditional shapes and methods of manufacture for their brass vessels, Chinese influence being restricted to the decoration, which was drawn from an assortment of different media.

The interior wall of a basin in the Victoria and Albert Museum bears figural scenes depicting an enthroned Mongol ruler with his attendants, all sporting looped hair and hats in typical Mongol fashion. The elaborate compositions – with groups of figures, some shown in three-quarter view, and landscape settings – show a sophisticated sense of draughtsmanship, which can be paralleled in the manuscript painting of Tabriz but was unknown to Persian painting before the Mongols arrived. The base of the same basin is decorated with roundels and panels containing swirling dragons, phoenixes, lotus and peony blossoms. These must have been inspired by Chinese decorative arts such as embroideries, which were greatly admired at the Mongol court.

75 Detail of a brass basin with flaring faceted sides, inlaid with silver and gold. The interior wall of the basin is decorated with scenes of Mongol court life in the same rectangular format and style as contemporary miniature painting. This detail shows a crowned ruler with attendants of the hunt. All the figures have the looped hair, tunics and boots fashionable at the Mongol court. Peonies and lotus blossoms, inspired by imported Chinese artefacts and textiles, fill the background as if growing wild.
DIAM (whole): 77 cm. Probably Tabriz, early 14th century.

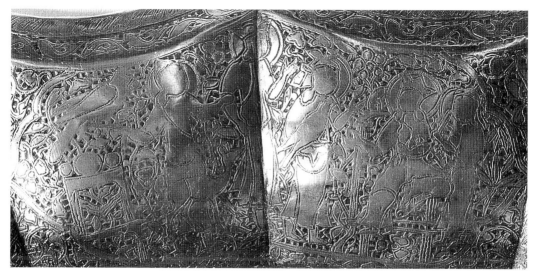

Unlike the ritual bronzes, Chinese silverwares were exported to the Middle East and were imitated by local metalworkers. They produced many silver cups and bowls, with engraved and gilt decoration and lobed or dragon-headed handles, which follow their Chinese prototypes closely in shape as well as decoration. Most surviving examples of these vessels are in the Hermitage, having been excavated from graves in the south-eastern area of the former USSR in territories occupied by the Mongols of the Golden Horde, but similar vessels were owned by their cousins in Iran and depicted in manuscript illustrations of this period.

A particularly productive school of metalwork, active throughout the fourteenth and into the fifteenth century, was based in the south of Iran in the province of Fars, probably at the capital Shiraz. Fars was ruled by the Injuid dynasty during the first half of the fourteenth century, and although the Injuids were defeated and replaced by the Muzaffarids in the 1350s, there is no noticeable break in the metalwork production of the area, nor indeed in its style.

76 OPPOSITE Silver bowl with a lobed handle, engraved with a lotus and other floral designs in Chinese style. It was found in a ruined tumulus in the Kochkor valley, east of Tashkent. DIAM: 14.5 cm. Central Asia, c.1300.

77 ABOVE Brass bowl inlaid with silver. The shape of the bowl and the titular inscription (see page 100) are comparable to Mamluk bowls of the same date (see fig. 89). DIAM: 24 cm. Shiraz, mid 14th century.

78 OPPOSITE Brass bowl
engraved with courtly
scenes, blessings and
verses and inlaid with
silver and gold. The
underside is decorated
with paired birds in
individual medallions
and the interior has a
complex design of fish
and other sea creatures.
DIAM: 17.8 cm. Shiraz,
late 14th century.

Fars metalwork is characterised by the use of bold inscriptions glorifying the sultan, who usually remains unnamed. The inscription on the bowl reads 'Glory to our lord, the most exalted, the most just, the most learned sultan, king that curbs nations, master of the sultans of the Arabs and the non-Arabs'. The titles are generally interspersed with courtly scenes of enthronement or sport, the swaying elongated figures distinctly reminiscent of contemporary miniature painting. Round-bottomed bowls such as this one were made in quantity, but other vessels include candlesticks, caskets, buckets and ewers.

Fars metalwork is remarkably consistent in terms of technique, form and style. Its attribution to Fars is founded on two examples in the Hermitage bearing the names of Injuid rulers whose titles include 'heir to the kingdom of Solomon'. This title was used by rulers of the province of Fars, and it recurs in inscriptions on several other objects which must also be of local manufacture. Surprisingly, the majority of these vessels bearing royal titles do not name any specific ruler, and it is therefore difficult to establish an internal chronology – variations in style may be due to different workshops rather than dates. However, the most complex and miniature designs probably date to the late fourteenth or even fifteenth century.

7

A group of stemmed cups made from high-tin bronze represent another school of metalwork in fourteenth-century Iran, although they have not been attributed to a specific centre. Lotus and peony blossoms are incorporated into the decoration and several cups are inscribed with esoteric verses relating to Alexander's quest for the source of life:

7

O sweet beverage of our pleasures
O transparent fount of mirth
If Alexander had not seen you
O world-revealing bowl of Mani's
How could his mind have conceived
The notion of the fount of life?

79 OPPOSITE Cauldron
of cast brass. This sort
of decorative cauldron
would have been
suitable for the outdoor
banquets popular
throughout the Islamic
period (see figs. 7 and
8). The three legs
enabled the cauldron to
be heated over a fire.
The contents could then
be poured out from the
spout or ladled in
smaller quantities.
DIAM: 62 cm. Khurasan,
14th century.

The metalwork of eastern Iran and Afghanistan after the Mongol invasions of the 1220s remains almost unknown. A group of large cast cauldrons helps to fill this gap. Although these vessels are primarily functional – the medieval equivalent of a soup tureen – the relief decoration can be very fine, with crouching animals supporting the handles and inscriptions on the flanges which often contain the signature of the craftsman. These cauldrons serve as a prelude to the massive water container made for the Great Mosque

79

at Herat in AH 776/AD 1374–5, and another even larger one commissioned by Timur for the shrine of Ahmad Yasavi, dated AH 801/AD 1399, which measures 1.58 × 2.43 metres.

The tendency to miniaturisation of the decoration, seen in the later metalwork of the Fars school, became much more pronounced during the fifteenth century. It was part of an aesthetic preference for more intricate designs that can be found in all the arts, compounded, no doubt, by the increased cost of gold and silver. Figures are omitted altogether in favour of abstract foliate designs executed in wire inlays. The inlayers maximised the effect of the precious metal by paring back the ground to leave it in slight relief.

In west Iran this style is characterised by the Mahmud al-Kurdi group, named after a craftsman whose signature appears on numerous objects. Mahmud al-Kurdi (the Kurd) and his colleagues used silver wire to create a rhythmical pattern, filling the enclosed areas with minute engraved arabesques and scrolls on a hatched ground. One advantage of this style of decoration was its flexibility, and it is found on objects of various shapes and sizes including buckets, trays, jugs, incense burners and hemispherical bowls with flat lids.

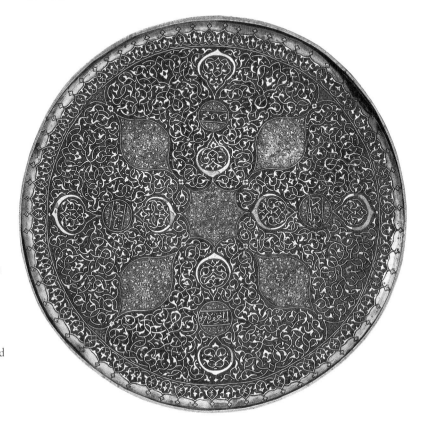

80 Dish of sheet brass engraved with an arabesque design and inlaid with silver and gold. The four small roundels contain the signature of the master inlayer Mahmud al-Kurdi, whose signature appears on many other objects. Different sizes of intricate arabesque interlace within fields delineated by thin wire and the use of a hatched ground are typical of his work. DIAM: 29 cm. North-west Iran, late 15th century.

In the past this group (as well as a large group of contemporary Mamluk metal wares) has been attributed to Muslim craftsmen working in Venice. There is little evidence to support this hypothesis, however, and stylistically the pieces fit quite happily within the body of Persian metalwork. It is more reasonable to assume that they were made, as both their style and Mahmud al-Kurdi's name suggest, in west Iran. However, they were certainly exported to Europe from Iran. Many have been preserved in European collections, some imitate European vessel shapes, and the Italian goldsmith Cellini and others are known to have admired Persian metalwork.

A similar aesthetic can be seen in the metalwork of Herat. Small
81 inscription panels compete with the foliate and arabesque designs, but the visual effect – of a complex and rhythmical surface pattern
82 with finely engraved intricate detail – is the same. Herat, founded by Timur in 1370, was an important artistic and literary centre under the Timurids. Contemporaries describe banquets with musical performances, poetry recitations, literary discussions,

81 Two jugs of cast brass inlaid with gold and silver. The fine arabesque decoration of the lidded jug is interspersed with Persian verses by Hafez. The other jug (missing its lid and handle) bears the name and titles of the Timurid ruler of Khurasan, Abu al-Ghazi Sultan Husayn (1470–1506). It is signed on the base by Muhammad ibn Shamsi of Ghur (east of Herat) and dated Sha'ban AH 903 (April 1498). HT (with lid): 16.5 cm. Herat, late 15th century.

82 OPPOSITE Dragon-headed candlestick of cast brass engraved with cartouches of racing animals. The dragon was a symbol of the lunar and solar eclipse in Islamic astrology and so was particularly appropriate for candle-holders: as the wax burnt down, the dragons appeared to swallow the two sources of light. HT: 25.5 cm. Khurasan, 15th century.

riddle solving and much wine drinking, and such parties are often depicted in illustrations to Timurid manuscripts. Drinking vessels used on these occasions included dragon-handled jugs of jade, porcelain and pottery as well as of metal. The inlaid brass jugs are often engraved with verses by Hafez and other poets which would have been particularly appropriate for such occasions. More than a hundred jugs of the same shape and dimensions, decorated in this style, are known. Many are signed by craftsmen whose names suggest that they came from Herat or the surrounding area, and enough are dated to establish that they were produced throughout the second half of the fifteenth and into the sixteenth century.

As gold and silver became more expensive during the fifteenth century, Chinese porcelains and tinned metal vessels began to threaten the position of inlaid brass as popular substitutes for precious metalwork. Porcelains had always been used at court, but during this period the number of imports rose sharply, and the Chinese even made vessels designed specifically for the Islamic market, some of them copying shapes developed in brass. Manuscript illustrations depict porcelains alongside gold and silver vessels at court, and they were obviously greatly prized.

The proliferation of tinned wares during the fifteenth century was probably generated by an increase in the availability (and decrease in the price) of tin, which was being imported from Europe once more. Tinning was not a new technique to the Middle East even though tin was not mined there. Cornish mines had supplied the eastern Roman empire with large quantities of tin, and tinning was common on the interiors of cooking and table wares before the collapse of Mediterranean trade in the sixth and seventh centuries.

Tin must have been used as a protective coating for copper-alloy cooking and table wares during the Islamic period also, otherwise their contents would have been foul-tasting and even poisonous. However, medieval writers suggest that tin was only imported from South-east Asia at this time. This would have inflated its price, thereby limiting its use for ordinary vessels and encouraging patrons to look to other non-precious materials such as pottery and glass. The cost of the metal may well be the reason why tinning is so rarely seen on surviving artefacts and why copper-alloy table and kitchen wares are not common.

As tin became more readily available there was a marked increase in the range and number of tablewares made from copper, brass and other copper alloys. The brass wine jugs, for example, would never have become so popular without tinned interiors, as the foul taste caused by the copper reacting to the acidic liquid could not have gone unnoticed.

83 Dish of cast copper, with engraved and tinned decoration of lotus flowers amidst Chinese cloud scrolls. Verses containing good wishes are inscribed around the cavetto and end with the date, AH 902/AD 1496–7. DIAM: 18.9 cm. Iran, 1496–7.

Tinned copper also provided an easier, cheaper and more realistic substitute for silver than did inlaid brass. Bowls, dishes, jugs and other vessels were manufactured in shapes which often imitated silverwork and were engraved with designs such as heavy-headed blossoms, animals in jungle-like foliage, cusped cartouches and other chinoiserie motifs which also decorated precious metal wares. Despite the decline of inlaid metalwork, these vessels appear to have drawn their buyers from lower down the social scale, for the individuals mentioned in their inscriptions are rarely identifiable. Without valuable gold and silver inlays these pieces were not considered prestigious enough for important figures of the court.

EGYPT AND SYRIA

85 OPPOSITE Penbox of brass inlaid with silver and gold. The radial inscription inside the lid contains the titles of an anonymous Mamluk amir. L: 30.7 cm. Damascus or Cairo, mid 14th century.

In 1250 the last Ayyubid sultan was overthrown by his own personal army and the Mamluk dynasty was founded in Cairo. The Mamluks ruled Egypt and Syria for more than 250 years and were responsible for evicting the last of the Crusaders and halting the western progress of the Mongols. They successfully defended the Mamluk empire from other incursions from the east, notably by Timur in 1400, and were never seriously threatened until their defeat by the mighty Ottoman army in 1517, when Egypt and Syria were swallowed by the vast Ottoman empire.

84 Steel mirror inlaid with silver and gold. The titles of the wife of an unnamed amir appear in the inscriptions. The blazon in the centre of the mirror, which represents the interior of a penbox with its separate compartments for pens and pots for ink and sand, suggests that the lady's husband occupied the post of secretary at court. DIAM: 21 cm. Cairo, mid 14th century.

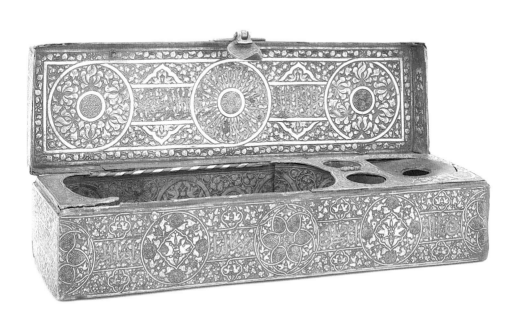

Mamluk can be translated as 'slave', and the Mamluks were, as their name indicates, a dynasty of slaves. However, there was nothing menial or degrading about becoming a Mamluk. On the contrary, it was the first stage of a potentially glittering career. Theoretically the Mamluks were a meritocracy, and with ability and luck a slave could rise to the highest office, even that of sultan. Imported when young, usually from Central Asia, Mamluk slave boys had no family or inherited land to divert their loyalty from their master and patron, and their status was entirely dependent on their position in the Mamluk hierarchy.

The Mamluk system had several distinct effects on metalwork and the other arts. Because the considerable wealth of the empire was concentrated in Mamluk hands, they were more important as patrons than the indigenous population. In addition, the emphasis on rank and position meant that titles and insignia of office played an increasingly important role in the decoration. It was not enough simply to possess the trappings of luxury and wealth – the individual's position in society had to be spelt out.

Huge quantities of gold and silver vessels, jewellery and horse trappings are said to have been found in the treasuries of the leading amirs of the fourteenth century. The sultans bestowed gold belts encrusted with gems on their favourite officers. Symbols of office, such as a penbox for the chief secretary and a cup for the cupbearer, were carried in processions by the highest-ranking amirs. No doubt they were as lavishly decorated as the Ottoman sultan's water flask, a rare surviving example of court regalia. The fate of this wealth of precious metal is described by the Mamluk historian Maqrizi. He describes people as so desperate for gold and silver during the economic turmoil of the later fourteenth century that they were prepared to pick it out from inlaid brass wares (vessels made of precious metal would have been melted down long before).

The lack of surviving gold and silver is more than made up for by the quantity of brass vessels, although many have indeed been deprived of their inlay. The quality of these wares and the number made for the sultan and leading amirs suggest that inlaid metalwork provided Mamluk goldsmiths with real competition. Sheet-brass metalworkers were able to reproduce the shapes of precious metal vessels, and the increase of zinc in the copper alloy gave the brass a golden hue that was frequently remarked upon by contemporaries. On occasion, inlaid brass may even have been preferred, both for its ability to display the Mamluk titles clearly and boldly and for the greater accuracy it allowed in the amirial blazons, which were differentiated by colour as well as design.

The inlay technique had become well established in Damascus

during the Ayyubid period. It seems to have spread to Cairo, the capital of the Mamluk empire, during the second half of the thirteenth century, probably in response to the demand of the Mamluk court, which was based there. Cairo and Damascus both remained important centres of the inlay technique, but at this stage it is often difficult to tell their products apart.

The types of objects produced and the manufacturing techniques used during the Mamluk period were, with few exceptions, the same as under Ayyubid rule. Candlesticks were made in particularly large quantities. Mamluk court ceremonial included candlelit processions when each amir would carry a candle, probably in one of these candlesticks. The candles were as finely decorated as their receptacles, with paper designs and gilding, and were probably almost as expensive.

86 Detail of a candlestick decorated with an amirial procession. One figure, carrying a penbox, was secretary at court (see figs. 84 and 85). Objects carried by the other figures probably also represent their positions at court. Their heads were 'cut off' at a later date by someone who clearly disapproved of figural decoration. Syria, 13th century.

87 Spherical brass incense burner pierced, engraved and inlaid with silver. The inscriptions (see opposite) include the name and titles of an important Mamluk amir, Badr al-Din Baysari, who died in prison in 1298. The gimbals inside prevented the incense from falling out when the burner rolled around the floor. DIAM: 18.4 cm. Damascus, 1264–79.

The greatest changes in Mamluk metalwork were not in the form or technique of the objects but in the style of the inlaid decoration. In the second half of the thirteenth century the influence of Mosul metalworkers is still apparent, and indeed several pieces are signed by craftsmen from Mosul. The surface is divided into friezes and roundels and the decoration is small in scale. Inscriptions consist of benedictions, but the main decoration is often figural: drinkers, musicians, huntsmen and personifications of the planets and zodiac on a scrolling ground.

Towards the end of the thirteenth century the taste of the predominantly Mamluk patrons begins to make itself felt. The blazons of the Mamluk amirs are often included within the decoration and the inscriptions usually list the self-glorifying amirial titles. The incense burner, made for one of the leading amirs of the early Mamluk period, is inscribed:

Made for the honourable authority, the high the lordly, the great amir, the esteemed, the masterly, the holy warrior, the defender, the protector of the frontiers, the fortified by God, the triumphant, the victorious Badr al-Din Baysari, al-Zahiri [officer of Sultan Baybars (1260–77)], al-Saʿidi [officer of Sultan Baraka Khan (1277–9)].

88 Large brass basin inlaid with silver and gold. The inscriptions contain the name and titles of Sultan Muhammad ibn Qalaun (d. 1341), and his epigraphic blazon, reading 'Glory to our Lord the Sultan', appears in the centre of the large roundels. The lotus flowers incorporated into the decoration indicate a date towards the end of the sultan's long reign, when Chinese influence was at its peak.
DIAM: 53.6 cm. Cairo or Damascus, 1330–41.

89 Bowl of sheet brass engraved and inlaid with silver. The inscriptions contain the titles of an anonymous amir of Sultan Muhammad ibn Qalaun (d.1341). Swimming fish engraved in the interior (RIGHT) suggest that these bowls were intended to hold water; they were probably used for ablutions. DIAM: 19.7 cm. Cairo or Damascus, early 14th century.

Favourite motifs include arabesques and flying birds; human figures, even astrological figures, become rare, perhaps because of increased religious sensitivity. For example, the internal bases of large basins, once decorated with figures of the planets and zodiac, are now invariably decorated with circling fish.

During the fourteenth century the egocentric tendencies of the Mamluk amirs become even more explicit on the metalwork they commissioned. Their titular inscriptions are larger and bolder, inlaid with wide areas of sheet silver so that their message cannot be missed. Radial inscriptions begin to appear in the roundels circling the blazon of the owner like rays of the sun – probably an intentional visual effect. The metalworker was forced to cram his other design ideas into the small amount of remaining space. Friezes of lotus and peony blossom suggest the influence of chinoiserie designs, also popular in Iran at this time.

The latter part of the fourteenth century was a turbulent period for the Mamluks. Political instability, civil wars, severe inflation and a series of plagues led to a drastic reduction in Mamluk patronage which lasted through the first half of the fifteenth century. The plagues must have killed craftsmen as well as patrons, and metalworkers were also beset by shortages of copper and silver which inflated the price of inlaid brass even further. Maqrizi, describing the Cairo inlay market in the 1430s, says, 'In our time inlaid brass has become little used by people and it is very rare to find it'.

Excavated material from a ship sunk off the Syrian coast (now in the Israel Museum, Jerusalem) provides important evidence to support Maqrizi's claim. The cargo contained a mass of copper coins, vessels and other objects. The coins, which were all minted in Syria before 1404, suggest that the ship sank around 1404/5 and that the metal wares were made in Syria during the latter part of the fourteenth century. The ship was probably bound for Cairo, which often demanded copper from Syria for the mint when there were shortages. No gold or silver coins were found, and the copper vessels are engraved but only one is inlaid.

Surviving inlaid brass objects from this period suggest that the metalworkers turned instead to the European market. A pointed European shield replaces the circular Mamluk blazon on many of these pieces, clearly revealing their destination, and a number are listed in the Medici and other European inventories from the late fifteenth century. The admiration which Europeans accorded Mamluk inlaid brass is well expressed by Simone Sigoli in his description of the markets of Damascus, which he visited in 1384–5:

90 OPPOSITE Jug of sheet brass engraved and inlaid with some silver and gold. The fine flame-tipped inscription contains the titles of an anonymous Mamluk sultan. The letters have double outlines as if intended for inlay but, despite its outstanding quality, this jug was only sparingly inlaid with silver and gold in the background. It was probably made during the latter part of the 14th century, when there was serious inflation as well as shortages of precious metal. The medallions contain sophisticated designs which were probably inspired by imported Chinese textiles. HT: 28.5 cm. Damascus or Cairo, late 14th century.

91 ABOVE Spouted bowl of cast brass inlaid with silver. The heraldic shield suggests that the bowl was intended for export to Europe even though the inscription contains Mamluk titles (see page 116). L: 23.5 cm. Damascus, late 14th century.

92 BELOW Bowl and incense burner of brass inlaid with silver and gold. These are typical of the vessels made specifically for the European market in the 15th century. Inventories suggest that the incense burners were used primarily as hand-warmers in the colder European climate. DIAM (bowl): 14 cm. Damascus, 15th century.

Here also is made a great deal of brass basins and pitchers and really they appear of gold, and then on the said basins and pitchers are made figures and foliage and other fine work in silver, so that it is a very beautiful thing to see.

At another point his admiration of the merchandise is such that he exclaims, 'Verily if you had money in the bone of your leg, without fail you would break it off to buy of these things'.

Metalwork had been made for export to Europe as early as the middle of the fourteenth century. For example, a large basin in the Louvre was made for Hugh IV of Lusignan, king of Cyprus (1324–59), and another in the Rijksmuseum, Amsterdam, bears the arms of Elizabeth of Hapsburg Carinthia, wife of Peter II of Sicily (1337–42). These were special commissions, with the patrons' titles in Arabic or Latin. Later in the century, as the trade with Europe increased, the metal vessels do not bear personalised titles and the European shields are left blank, to be completed on purchase.

At first the metalworkers reproduced the types of metal vessels they were accustomed to making for their Mamluk patrons. The pouring bowl, a type popular with Mamluk amirs since the early fourteenth century, is an example of this transitional stage. The metalworker has even retained the usual amirial titles:

The high authority, the lordly, the possessing, the just, the diligent, the learned, the holy warrior, the defender, the protector of the frontiers, the possessing, the just [the amir of] al-Malik al-Nasir.

These titles were obviously inappropriate for a non-Mamluk patron, and gradually the inscriptions on export wares were adapted. Single innocuous titles such as 'the possessor' were repeated in a meaningless way on later vessels. After a time even the pretence of legibility was dropped and the inscriptions became purely ornamental letter forms with plaited and knotted shafts.

The new market was swift to demand different vessels. The Venetian merchants who dominated Mediterranean trade evidently returned to the workshops with specific requests for vessels that would sell well in Europe. Several types were made for the first time during the late fourteenth and the fifteenth century, most bearing European shields: hemispherical bowls with flat lids, small candlesticks with flaring rims, spherical incense burners and trays.

A revival of Mamluk patronage of inlaid metalwork occurred during the long reign of Sultan Qaitbay (1468–96), and some of the pieces produced for the sultan are extremely fine, with extensive gold and silver inlay. However, these exquisite pieces appear to

93 Tray of sheet brass engraved and inlaid with silver. The shape of this tray (or paten), with its raised centre to support the base of a ewer (or chalice), is European, and the coat of arms (superimposed on a shield of the same shape) indicates that it was destined for Europe. A number of these trays with almost identical decoration are known. Confronted phoenixes and elaborate lotus blossoms were also popular motifs on textiles exported to Venice. DIAM: 55 cm. Damascus, *c.*1400.

have been produced on a small scale, perhaps solely for the court in Cairo. Other vessels made for him and his family are restrained in their use of inlays, and it is rare for non-royal objects to have any.

As in Iran, tinning became increasingly popular during the fifteenth century, and Mamluk patrons welcomed these cheaper imitations of the silver wares and inlaid brasses that they could not afford. The majority of the tinned objects are lunch boxes, plates, large dishes and other tablewares; like their Persian colleagues, the Mamluk metalworkers appreciated the protective coating against verdigris that tinning provided. The engraved decoration on these vessels often includes amirial titles and blazons, and some bear names which can be identified with amirs based in Syria. While there are general stylistic resemblances to the Qaitbay group, these objects are of inferior quality, both in materials and in execution, and were probably produced away from the court in Damascus.

Inlaid metalwork of the fourteenth century is unsurpassed in communicating its message clearly and effectively; Islamic base metalwork never regained that sense of purpose and visual impact. Fifteenth-century pieces, with their intricate designs and narrow wire inlays, signal the victory of virtuosity over design, and the potential was soon exhausted.

94 RIGHT Ewer of sheet brass engraved and sparingly inlaid with silver, made for the wife of Sultan Qaitbay (1472–96). The titular inscription is not inlaid. Instead the brass is polished to give a golden effect.
HT: 47 cm. Cairo, 1472–96.

95 OPPOSITE Lunch box of brass, engraved and originally tinned. It consists of three round containers, which fit one on top of the other, and a lid which doubles as a lunch bowl. Originally, metal shafts fitted down both sides kept the parts together and even locked if it were felt necessary (food poisoning was a favourite Mamluk method of assassination). The cartouches contain a poem popular on Mamluk metal objects of this period.
HT: 18.4 cm. Damascus, 15th century.

The decline of the inlay technique makes 1500 a convenient year at which to break off this short history of Islamic metalwork. The sixteenth century saw the rise of the three empires – Ottoman, Safavid and Mughal – which were to dominate the Islamic world into the modern period. Increased trade across the globe encouraged the use of imported rare materials and vessels at court, as rulers vied with one another for the most extravagant and cosmopolitan display. Henceforth, royal patronage of metalwork was concentrated on the lavish gold vessels encrusted with gems, rock crystal, jade and other valuable materials which are still visible in the treasury of the Topkapi Palace in Istanbul.

Inlaid brass did not disappear completely; in fact it was successfully revived in Cairo and Damascus in the nineteenth century and the technique adapted for use on steel objects and Mughal *bidri* ware. However, plain or engraved brass, steel and tinned or gilded copper became the most common alternatives to gold and silver for those patrons who could not afford precious metal, or for objects for which gold and silver were inappropriate. At their best these later metal wares are bold and impressive, but without gold and silver inlays court interest in base-metal vessels subsided and they were rarely commissioned as items of prestige and display. After three hundred years of extraordinary success as a material demanded by patrons of the highest rank, brass and other base metals returned to their former place in the material hierarchy: providing simple functional objects and cheaper imitations of precious metalwork.

96 Steel peacock engraved with figural scenes and inscriptions, with some gilded decoration and gold overlay; the bird's eyes are set with turquoises. ʿAli, the fourth caliph and first Shiite imam, and his two sons, Hasan and Husain, are depicted in the central medallion on the fanned tail. HT: 89 cm. Iran, 19th century.

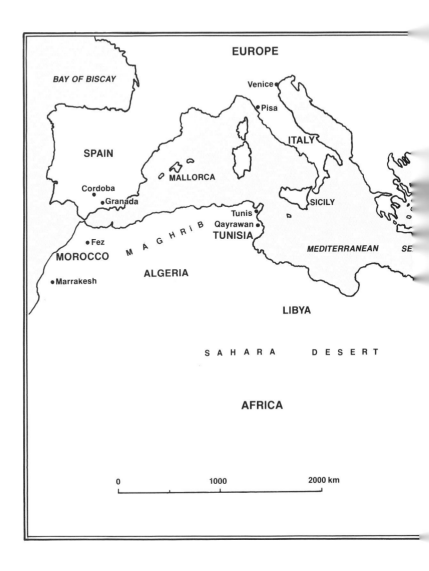

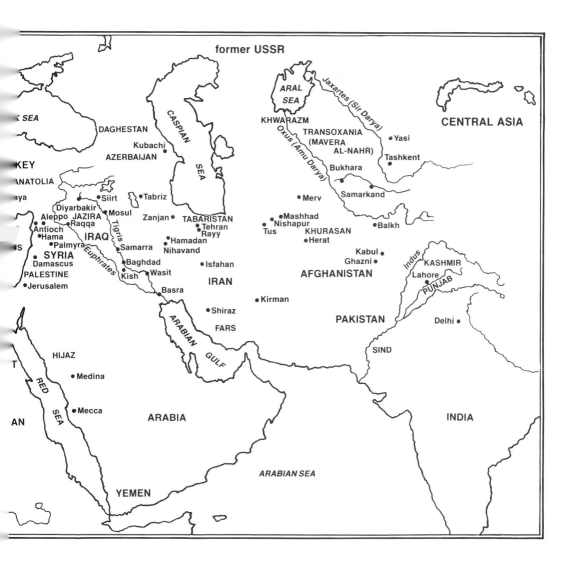

THE ISLAMIC WORLD

FURTHER READING

The following is not intended as a full bibliography. The most easily available publications, with a heavy bias towards those written in English, are listed below, but only the most important or relevant articles in scholarly journals have been included and none of the extensive literature written in Russian. Books with good bibliographies have been marked with an asterisk (*) and the reader is referred to these for more complete lists.

Allan, J.W., 'Silver: The key to bronze in early Islamic Iran', *Kunst des Orients* 11, 1976–7, pp. 5–21.
Analyses the relationship between base and precious metalwork and suggests that a silver shortage inspired the use of inlaid brass.

Allan, J.W., *Persian Metal Technology 700–1300 AD*, Oxford, 1979.*
Useful survey based on information from medieval texts.

Allan, J.W., *Nishapur: Metalwork of the early Islamic period*, New York, 1982.*
Rare opportunity to assess the range of metalwork used in a medieval Persian town.

Allan, J.W., *Islamic Metalwork: The Nuhad Es-Said collection*, London, 1982.*
Fabulously illustrated catalogue with detailed discussion of individual objects.

Allan, J.W., *Metalwork of the Islamic World: The Aron collection*, London, 1986.*
Well-illustrated catalogue preceded by a series of essays.

Atil, E., Chase, W. and Jett, P., *Islamic Metalwork in the Freer Gallery of Art*, Washington, DC, 1985.*
Includes technical analysis of the manufacture and decoration of each object.

Baer, E., *Metalwork in Medieval Islamic Art*, New York, 1983.*
Organised by object type and by decorative themes.

Baer, E., *Ayyubid Metalwork with Christian Images*, Leiden, 1989.
Survey, discussion and bibliography of thirteenth-century metalwork with Christian iconography.

Barrett, D., *Islamic Metalwork in the British Museum*, London, 1949.
Out of print, but a good short introduction to the subject.

Craddock, P. and Lang, J., 'Spinning, turning, polishing', *Historical Metallurgy* 17/2, 1983, pp. 79–81.

Earliest evidence of spun metal-work in thirteenth-century Mosul.

Craddock, P., La Niece, S. and Hook, D., 'Brass in the medieval Islamic world', in 2000 Years of Zinc and Brass (ed. P. Craddock), London, 1990, pp. 73–99.
Includes analyses of the metal composition of many objects.

Fehérvári, G., Islamic Metalwork of the Eighth to the Fifteenth Century in the Keir Collection, London, 1976.*
Useful catalogue of an important private collection.

Hartner, W., 'The Vaso Vescovali in the British Museum', Kunst des Orients 9, 1973–4, pp. 99–130.
Detailed study of Islamic astrological iconography.

The Israel Museum, From the Depths of the Sea, Jerusalem, 1985.
Includes metal wares from a shipwreck of c.1400.

University of Michigan, Sasanian Silver, Ann Arbor, Michigan, 1967.
Introduction by Oleg Grabar quotes early Arab poetry in praise of Sasanian silver.

Mango, M. Mundell, Silver from Early Byzantium: The Kaper Karaon and related treasure, Baltimore, 1986.
Illustrates the range of Byzantine silver before the Arab conquest.

Marçais, G. and Poinssot, L., Objets Kairouanais IXe au XIIIe siècle, vol. II, Tunis, 1952.
Important evidence of North African metalworking tradition.

Marschak, B., Silberschätze des Orients, Leipzig, 1986.*
Early Islamic silver and its relationship to pre-Islamic cultures.

Melikian-Chirvani, A.S., Islamic Metalwork from the Iranian World, 8th–18th centuries (Victoria and Albert Museum catalogue), London, 1982.*
Comprehensive study by leading authority on Persian metalwork.

Melikian-Chirvani, A.S., 'Silver in Islamic Iran: The evidence from literature and epigraphy', Oxford Studies in Islamic Art III, 1986, pp. 89–107.
Useful survey of medieval references to precious metalwork.

Pope, A.U., A Survey of Persian Art, 6 vols, Oxford, 1938–9.
Good illustrations of objects in this influential exhibition.

Rice, D.S., 'The brasses of Badr al-Din Lu'lu', Bulletin of the School of Oriental and African Studies 14, 1952, pp. 564–78.

Rice, D.S., 'Studies in Islamic Metalwork I–VI', Bulletin of the School of Oriental and African Studies 14, 15, 17, 20 and 21, 1952–8.

Rice, D.S., 'Inlaid brasses from the workshop of Ahmad al-Dhaki al-Mawsili', Ars Orientalis 2, 1957, pp. 283–326.

Pioneering studies especially important for the Mosul and Syrian schools of inlaid brass.

Rogers, J.M. and Ward, R.M., Süleyman the Magnificent, London, 1988.*
Exhibition catalogue with illustrations of court regalia from Ottoman Turkey.

ILLUSTRATION ACKNOWLEDGEMENTS

INDEX